Ways to use this prayer guide

We pray better together.
Over 150,000 believers from many hundreds of churches will be praying these prayers. So you won't be praying alone. Encourage someone you know to join with you by using the app (see below), or by giving them a copy of the booklet.

Find and share practical ideas.
Check out the resources at waymakers.org. Find practical ways to remind your church family to pray, such as bulletin inserts and powerpoint slides. Interact with others about what you like in the prayers at Facebook.com/seekgodforthecity.

Pray with the Spanish translation.
Invite Spanish-speaking friends to pray with *Seek God for the City* in Spanish. It's called *Clama a Dios por la Ciudad 2016*. The 64-page booklet is available at the same low cost as the English version. Available December 2015.

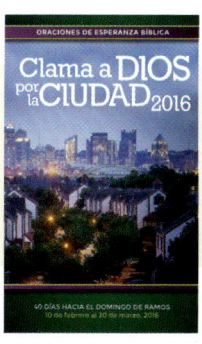

Pray with the kids: A children's version.
Download the kid's version in "pdf" format at no cost from our website. It's a great resource to engage kids in this prayer adventure! Find it at **waymakers.org**.

Pray as you go: Get the companion app.
Download the *Seek God 2016* app on your tablet or smartphone. The app contains all of the same scriptures, prayers and helpful material. The app makes it even more flexible and accessible. Available December 2015. Only 99¢. Learn more at **waymakers.org**. Tell your friends in other cities and countries about the app.

iOS Android

One City's Story of Hope

Days of Hope for San Diego

As Christians from diverse churches pray together, God often gives them ways to work together with a vision of Christ's kingdom, bringing life, renewal and blessing to every dimension of their city.

Many are encouraged to see God's people pursue the hope of Christ's kingdom as they fulfill their God-given roles in matters of business and functions of government. One such movement has gained momentum in recent years, beginning in east San Diego, California.

The story began more than 30 years ago, when several pastors in east San Diego found ways to pray together. Many of them have gathered monthly for years, building long-lasting relationships.

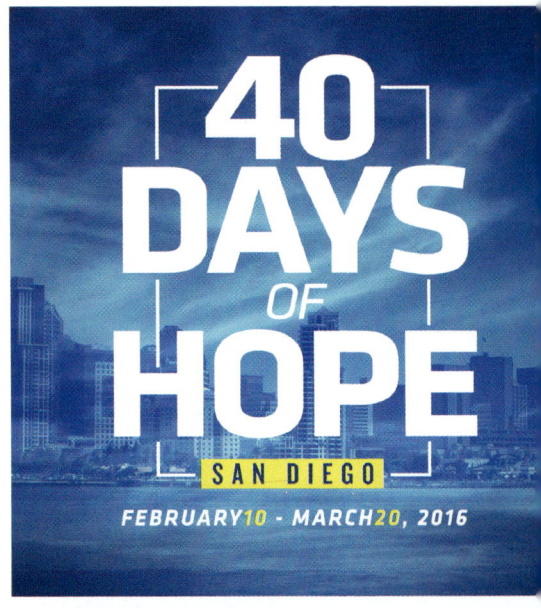

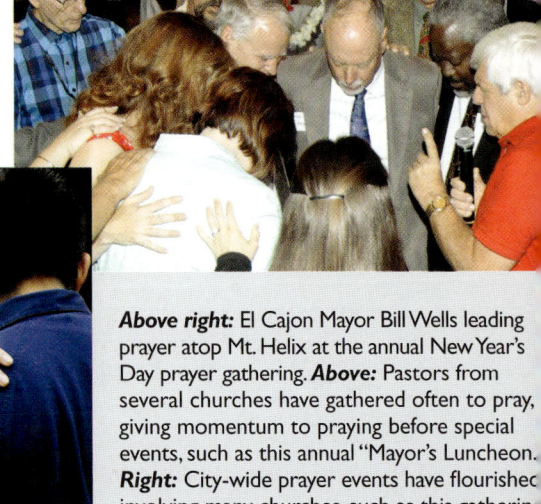

Above right: El Cajon Mayor Bill Wells leading prayer atop Mt. Helix at the annual New Year's Day prayer gathering. **Above:** Pastors from several churches have gathered often to pray, giving momentum to praying before special events, such as this annual "Mayor's Luncheon." **Right:** City-wide prayer events have flourished involving many churches, such as this gathering on the morning of New Year's Day, 2015.

Praying in Unity, Serving in Love

In 2013, El Cajon mayor Bill Wells, a dedicated Christian, made a special request of pastors and Christian leaders. The mayor asked if the churches of the city would organize a season of sustained prayer specifically for the Second Street area.

Pastors responded. A simple plan was formed. It would be called "40 Days of Hope for 2nd Street." During each one of the 40 days, prayerwalking teams were organized to pray Christ's blessing on every business, school and home in the 2nd Street area.

Prayerwalking teams readily offered to pray for residents and homeless, business owners and shoppers. Daily prayer prompts, published on a website, focused the prayers of many more.

City leaders calling for help with Christians putting feet to their prayers.

3

Praying, Walking and Working

Walking in hope in East San Diego..

During the 40 days, over 200 prayerwalking teams–with people from 25 churches–set out, offering personal prayer to more than 1000 people. There were tangible outcomes: A measurable increase in commerce during and after the season was noticed. Police had to deal with fewer problems. An adult bookstore permanently closed on the 39th day.

Pastors, government and business leaders, impressed with the fruit of collaborating in prayer and service, called for additional 40 day seasons in 2014 and 2015. Many began fasting during the 40 days with pastors meeting together daily for prayer as congregations partnered together in community prayer gatherings and evangelism.
In 2015 the 40 days ended with "Love Week" when everyone was encourage to perform random acts of kindness in the community.

Together for Christ's Kingdom

..leads to uniting in hope throughout the region

Pastors of churches, government leaders and business owners have been paying attention to what has been happening in the eastern part of greater San Diego. Plans have emerged for the "40 Days of Hope" to move far beyond El Cajon's 2nd Street to involve people throughout greater San Diego. Organizers are calling it simply, "Unite San Diego."

Hopes are high that seasons of united prayer will inspire and empower God's people to pray and labor in practical hope for Christ's life-giving power to abound in affairs of government, the market place and ultimately, to every street, school, business and home of greater San Diego.

Churches praying and co-laboring with government and business leaders

Photo by James Blank

In 2016, the "40 Days of Hope" will begin on February 10, and continue through March 20. Some churches plan on using *Seek God for the City* as a guide to prompt united prayer. Many will be fasting. See **40daysofhope.net** to follow this year and in years to come.

Seeking His **Life** to **Revive** the Church

FEBRUARY 10-20 WEEK 1

This "week" (actually an 11-day period, beginning on Ash Wednesday, February 10) we will pray toward the hope that God will revive His people with spiritual life.

As you pray for God's people in your city, you will be praying these same prayers with thousands of others who are praying for God's life in their communities. As you pray for your own church, be sure to pray for the life and unity of other churches. Pray that together, God's people would freshly experience the splendor of His power and His life so that we become Christ's instruments to complete His purposes throughout the earth.

The **Americas** and the **Caribbean**

During the 40 days, we will pray for the continental areas of the earth in reverse sequence of Acts 1:8. Thus, we begin at one of the areas of the earth farthest from Jerusalem. We'll start by praying for the continents of South and North America and the Caribbean.

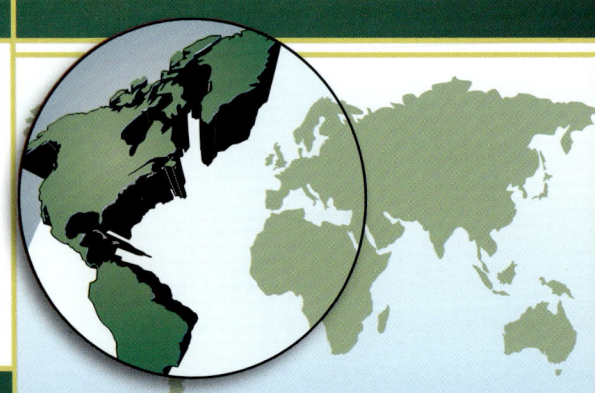

SEEK GOD
...for His reviving life to bring joy

Day 1
WEDNESDAY
FEBRUARY 10

You forgave the iniquity of Your people;
You covered all their sin…
Restore us, O God of our salvation…
Will You not Yourself revive us again,
that Your people may rejoice in You?
— Psalm 85:2, 4, 6

We stand together before You as Your people. We acknowledge that among us there are sins great and small. We are grateful for the free forgiveness in Christ that covers such sins. But You have saved us for a greater purpose than merely managing our cycles of sin. Haven't You saved us so that we might serve You in the ever-new life of Your risen Son? Revive us in ways that change us deeply. Infuse us with the resurgent life of Your Spirit, so that we find ourselves rejoicing in rising, always-escalating love for Your Son.

His father saw him and felt compassion…
the son said to him, "Father, I have sinned against heaven and in your sight."
…But the father said to his slaves,
"Quickly bring out the best robe…
let us eat and celebrate;
for this son of mine was dead
and has come to life again."…
And they began to celebrate. — Luke 15:20-24

Why are we surprised that Your heart overflows in party-starting joy whenever a long lost son or daughter comes home? Whenever we turn toward You, even slightly, we find that You have already been seeking us. What vigilant love! What extravagant gladness! To come home to You, to sense Your delight, is like coming back to life from the dead. Make us jubilant in Your house so that many more in our city will find their way home to You. *Pray:*

- For many who only know of God's forgiveness to also experience His life-giving power.
- For God's joy to be revealed with His love, so that many come home to Him.

Seek God on behalf of **Children**

That children will hear the gospel and encounter Christ early in life; that God's great fatherly heart will be revealed with healing power to kids who have been wounded or disappointed by their parents; for lasting family stability; for excellence in education; for wisdom to be formed in their early days; for safety from violence and perversion; for laughter and joy.

PRAYERWALK: Pray for kids in your neighborhood or pray near schools and playgrounds in any part of town. Pray for the entire family that surrounds children that you see.

Let the little children come to Me, and do not hinder them, for the kingdom of God belongs to such as these.
— Mark 10:14 (NIV)

Seek God on behalf of **the Americas and the Caribbean**
Anguilla, Antigua and Barbuda, Argentina, Aruba, Bahamas

SEEK GOD
...for the revealing of God's love

Day 2
THURSDAY
FEBRUARY 11

*Show us Your lovingkindness, O LORD,
  and grant us Your salvation.
I will hear what God the LORD will say;
  for He will speak peace to His people,
  to His godly ones;
but let them not turn back to folly.*
— Psalm 85:7-8

*He who has My commandments
  and keeps them is the one who loves Me.
And he who loves Me
  will be loved by My Father,
  and I will love him
  and will disclose Myself to him.*
— John 14:21

We find ourselves turning back to stubborn habits of heart again and again. It is folly to imagine that we will be changed by merely deciding to be different. Only You can change us. Reveal the magnificent love of Christ as never before. Save us in ways we have not expected. Give us ears that listen for Your voice, speaking Your life-changing word in ways that bring about a deep and lasting difference. Declare Your peace with such power that we are transfigured to live in the fullness of Christ's life.

Lord Jesus, You know our hearts. You see all of our sincere but still erratic efforts to serve You. Disclose Your love to us so that we know Your heart toward us. Even our feeble attempts to obey You end up delighting You because of Your vast, forever love. We have perceived only the smallest glimpse of Your mighty kindness. As You promised, show us more and more of Yourself. The more we experience Your love, the more we will find ourselves obeying You with joy. *Pray:*

- For the enormity of God's love to be revealed to many of your city.
- For Christ to encounter struggling believers with heart-changing clarity, so that they live in the power of His love.

Seek God on behalf of **Homeless People**

Pray for immediate relief, shelter, food and health care; that Christ will restore hope for the future; for wise counsel and trustworthy friendship; for protection from the risks of life on the streets; for employment, housing and restored family life.

PRAYERWALK: Visit a place where homeless people seek shelter or employment. Pray God's blessing on the people you see who appear to be homeless.

But He lifted the needy out of their affliction and increased their families like flocks.
— Psalm 107:41 (NIV)

Seek God on behalf of **the Americas and the Caribbean**
Barbados, Belize, Bermuda, Bolivia, Brazil

SEEK GOD
...for revival bringing salvation and glory

Day 3
FRIDAY
FEBRUARY 12

*Surely His salvation is near
  to those who fear Him,
that glory may dwell in our land.*
— Psalm 85:9

We are familiar with the truth that Jesus is our Savior. Now bring us into a deeper encounter with Jesus as the Living One, risen from the dead, presiding now in our midst. Fill our hearts with awe concerning the purpose of Your Son. You have saved us for more than merely having a better life and a brighter afterlife. You have saved us so that we might walk, breathe and speak like You–that Your glory would be seen in our lives and in our land. No longer will we postpone the hope of Your glory until the age to come. We pray for You to advance Your purpose in us now. Continually save us and fill us in these days, so that we reflect Your love and glory.

*Martha said to Him,
  "I know that he will rise again
  in the resurrection on the last day."
Jesus said to her,
  "I am the resurrection and the life...
  Did I not say to you that if you believe,
  you will see the glory of God?"*
— John 11:24-25, 40

Yes, we believe that we will see the glory of God in our day. We believe in You. You are the Risen One. You were raised from death, but You are more than resurrection. You are life itself. Bring Your life to many, and with Your life, show Your brilliant glory. *Pray:*

- For believers to be filled with renewed hope to envision and to experience the singular glory of Jesus in our day.
- That many would trust in Christ, and by faith, receive His life and behold His glory.

Seek God on behalf of **Women**

That women will be honored in their unique, God-created glory; that every kind of injustice toward women will cease; for pornography to be stopped; for protection from sexual violence; that hope would be renewed for the beauty of marriage and children; that single women would lay hold of God's full purpose in their lives.

PRAYERWALK: Pray prayers of blessing for some of the women you come in contact with today.

This woman was abounding with deeds of kindness and charity which she continually did.
— Acts 9:36

Seek God on behalf of **the Americas and the Caribbean**
British Virgin Islands, Canada, Cayman Islands, Chile, Colombia

SEEK GOD
...for revival bringing righteousness and peace

Day 4
SATURDAY
FEBRUARY 13

*Righteousness and peace
   have kissed each other.
Truth springs from the earth,
   and righteousness looks down from heaven.
Indeed, the LORD will give what is good,
   and our land will yield its produce.
Righteousness will go before Him
   and will make His footsteps into a way.*
   – Psalm 85:10-13

You have intended for the life of Christ to be planted and to thrive throughout our city. But many of us have gone fallow, so that we are untended, wild and fruitless. Sow the seed of the truth into many minds and lives. Come like the sun with Your power. Come like the rain by Your Spirit. Cultivate our community, patiently bringing forth lives marked by Christ's righteousness. Cause Your presence to come upon us, as if You were walking ahead of us, step by step marking out a way of living that abounds with the fruit of Your kingdom.

*For you will...prepare His ways;
   to give to His people
   the knowledge of salvation
      by the forgiveness of their sins...
to guide our feet into the way of peace.*
   – Luke 1:76-77, 79

It was promised that when You came, Lord Jesus, many would experience forgiveness of sins. And so it came to pass; and so it continues today. But Your salvation comes with a further promise, that we would learn how to live in the might and joy of heaven's peace. Visit us in peace-bringing power. Guide us step by step to walk in Your ways, and gradually bring lasting transformation to our entire community. *Pray:*

- For Christ-followers to experience His guiding presence as never before.
- For believers to walk in the righteousness of God, influencing the economy, values and character of their community.

Seek God on behalf of **Single People**

Pray that Christ will fill singles' hearts with His love; that they may taste the satisfaction which is found only in God; that friendships will bring ample fullness of relationship; for sexual purity and simplicity of lifestyle; and strong marriages for those who desire them. Pray for those single by divorce or death, that they would find healing and new hope for life ahead.

PRAYERWALK: Bless those who are single in your neighborhood. Consider their story. Pray for their future and hopes.

One who is unmarried is concerned about the things of the Lord, how he may please the Lord.
   – 1 Corinthians 7:32

Seek God on behalf of **the Americas and the Caribbean**
Costa Rica, Cuba, Dominica, Dominican Republic, Ecuador

SEEK GOD
...to restore His people to fruitfulness

Day 5
SUNDAY
FEBRUARY 14

Turn again, O God of hosts;
  look down from heaven, and see;
have regard for this vine,
  the stock that Your right hand planted...
But let Your hand be upon the one...
  whom You made strong for Yourself.
Then we will never turn back from You.
Give us life, and we will call on Your name.
— Psalm 80:14-15, 17-18 (NRSV)

We are like a hand-planted garden in Your sight. Like a vineyard keeper watches his vineyard, You constantly examine us. You intend for us to bloom with Your beauty and multiply Your life in others. We are alive, but often fruitless. We have produced little more than leaves. Do not merely look on us from afar. Come near to us. Extend Your hand, the very hand that formed us, in order to restore us. Stretch us and strengthen us to grow in Your glory, presenting to You the lasting fruit of families and friends who praise Your name.

I am the true vine,
  and My Father is the vinedresser.
Every branch in Me that does not bear fruit,
He takes away [original language: He lifts] ...
I am the vine, you are the branches;
  he who abides in Me and I in him,
  he bears much fruit. — John 15:1-2, 5

You have destined us to bear much fruit, yet You often find us barren. Father, lift us from the ground, where some of us lie dry and dormant in the shadows. Stretch us upward, staking us and holding us open before the light of heaven. May the power of Christ's life course through us to bring forth all that pleases You. *Pray:*

- For despondent or fruitless believers to be lifted into the light of God's presence.
- For Christians to be stretched in spiritual disciplines in order to serve in God's purposes.

Seek God on behalf of International Visitors

For students, workers and businesspeople from other lands to be treated with honor and respect; that they will enjoy new friendships; that they will encounter the message of the gospel clearly declared and lovingly demonstrated.

PRAYERWALK: Find a public place or business which draws international visitors or students. As you see people from different nations, pray God's blessing on them and their home countries.

Assemble the people –men, women and children, and the aliens living in your towns– so they can listen and learn to fear the LORD your God.
— Deuteronomy 31:12 (NIV)

Seek God on behalf of the Americas and the Caribbean
El Salvador, Falkland Islands, French Guiana, Greenland

SEEK GOD
...to impart His life-giving Spirit

Day 6
MONDAY
FEBRUARY 15

*"Son of man, can these bones live?"
I answered, "O Lord GOD, You know."...
"Behold, I will cause breath to enter you
 that you may come to life."...
So I prophesied as He commanded me,
 and the breath came into them,
 and they came to life
 and stood on their feet...
"I will put My Spirit within you
 and you will come to life."*
– Ezekiel 37:3, 5, 10, 14

We pray today for those who are physically alive but are spiritually dead. Breathe life into them, as You did at creation. Infuse them with Your Spirit. As Ezekiel did so long ago, we declare our prayer: "Come to life! He will put His Spirit within you and you will come to life!" Come upon us, Spirit of God! Resuscitate those who have suffocated in their sin. Renew many who have wavered in their love for You. Surprise some who have not yet known You. Raise up great throngs of people throughout the earth to stand before You, filled with life and eager to serve.

*Truly, truly, I say to you,
 an hour is coming and now is,
 when the dead will hear
 the voice of the Son of God,
and those who hear will live.* – John 5:25

People who are spiritually dead have been coming to life by Your word since the day You rose from the grave. We pray that many more in our city will hear Your voice and live by the power of the gospel. Only Your voice gives life. A whisper from You can wake our lifeless friends. One word can rouse our sleeping churches. A shout can raise many throughout our city. Lift Your voice, Son of God! Raise many to fullness of life. *Pray:*

- For many who are far from God to hear His word and receive His life-giving Spirit.
- For struggling or dying churches to be renewed in Christ's life.

Seek God on behalf of **Gangs**

That God will satisfy their deep desires for significance and belonging; for God to break the spiritual and social powers that hold them; for caring Christians to embrace them in the authentic love of God's family; for blessing upon the neighborhoods they claim.

PRAYERWALK: Pray at a place affected by gang activity. Speak God's Word as you walk to spiritually "tag" the territories with unseen but real declarations of Christ's lordship, love and blessing.

*Help, LORD, for the godly
man ceases to be, for the
faithful disappear from
among the sons of men...
"Now I will arise,"
says the LORD,
"I will set him in the
safety for which he longs."*
– Psalm 12:1, 5

Seek God on behalf of **the Americas and the Caribbean**
Grenada, Guadeloupe, Guatemala, Guyana, Haiti

SEEK GOD
...for Christ's resurrection power

Day 7
TUESDAY
FEBRUARY 16

Come, let us return to the LORD.
  For He has torn us,
    but He will heal us;
He has wounded us,
  but He will bandage us.
He will revive us after two days;
He will raise us up on the third day,
  that we may live before Him.
— Hosea 6:1-2

Our sin has grieved You greatly. It has harmed us far more than we have realized. You have allowed the consequences of our sin to fall upon us. Wounded, we ran from You, blaming You for our pain. Even so, You have preserved us for a time of returning to You. May this be the time of turning and a day of healing for many of our city. The healing of our broken souls may not happen instantly. Give us hope to wait patiently for Your healing to renew us fully. Surely You will revive those You love, so that we no longer run from You, but live before You with face-to-face nearness.

When I saw Him,
  I fell at His feet like a dead man.
And He placed His right hand on me,
  saying, "Do not be afraid;
    I am the first and the last,
    and the living One;
  and I was dead, and behold,
  I am alive forevermore,
and I have the keys of death and of Hades."
— Revelation 1:17-18

Lord Jesus, You are the Living One, alive with a different kind of life. A mere glimpse of Your glory caused Your closest friend to collapse at Your feet as if he were dead. But You touched him and spoke to him, forbidding him to fear. Place Your hand upon us as well, Living One. Speak to our hearts and lift us from our fears. Use the keys in Your hand to unlock the doors of death that hold many of our city in darkness. *Pray:*

- For believers to recognize the risen Jesus in the beauty of His glory.
- For the authority of Christ to liberate people from the grip of sin, the fear of death and the deception of evil powers.

Seek God on behalf of **Marriages**

Thank God for sturdy marriages that reflect His faithfulness and beauty. Pray especially for marriages which are strained to a breaking point or are failing, that God will bring both hope and help; that He will heal broken hearts and restore intimacy; for every marriage, that God will refresh and re-center homes in Christ.

PRAYERWALK: Pray for the married couples living in your neighborhood.

Marriage should be honored by all.
— Hebrews 13:4 (NIV)

Seek God on behalf of **the Americas and the Caribbean**
Honduras, Jamaica, Martinique, Mexico, Montserrat

SEEK GOD
...to purify His people

Day 8
WEDNESDAY
FEBRUARY 17

Purify me with hyssop,
*   and I shall be clean.*
Wash me,
*   and I shall be whiter than snow...*
Create in me a clean heart, O God,
*   and renew a steadfast spirit within me.*
                  – Psalm 51:7, 10

We have tried to find ways to erase feelings of guilt and shame. But doing self-help therapy or adding religious fervency sometimes does no more than darken the stains of our sin. We renounce the preposterous idea that we could ever make ourselves pure. Make us clean. Free us from the lingering power of sin. Wash away the sense of disgrace and distance from You. Give us confidence that we are pleasing before You. Renew us as a people from the inside so that we are strong and steady to serve You in our day.

Blessed are the pure in heart,
for they shall see God.
                  – Matthew 5:8

We are conflicted by self-absorbed pride and self-accusing shame. Do Your work, Lord Jesus. We might not ever lift our eyes toward You unless You purify our hearts. Simplify the mix of motives that drives our lives. Clear the clutter of competing desires. Give us a simple, single-hearted passion for You. Align our scattered thoughts and focus our hopes so that the only thing that matters is that You alone will be seen and loved by all. *Pray:*

- For non-believers to see the hope of whole-hearted purity before God.
- For believers to confess and abandon patterns of sin in order to walk in the joy of holiness.

Seek God on behalf of **Sick People**

That God will touch those who are sick in your community with healing and comfort; that they will grow in grace as God walks with them throughout their ordeal; that God will provide for their financial needs; for their caregivers and families; that many will renew their trust in Christ and follow Him boldly, even in affliction.

    PRAYERWALK: Consider those who may be struggling with chronic illness or pain in your neighborhood. Pray for their healing.

He saw a large crowd, and felt compassion for them and healed their sick.
       – Matthew 14:14

Seek God on behalf of **the Americas** and the **Caribbean**
Netherlands Antilles, Nicaragua, Panama, Paraguay, Peru

SEEK GOD
...for His people to love and obey Him

Day 9
THURSDAY
FEBRUARY 18

*I have set before you life and death...
So choose life in order that you may live
...by loving the LORD your God,
by obeying His voice,
and by holding fast to Him;
for this is your life
and the length of your days.*
— Deuteronomy 30:19-20

If all You wanted was perfect performance, You could easily commandeer our minds and program our souls to obey You with never-failing precision. But instead of robotic religious behavior, You desire genuine love that chooses to serve You freely. We have chosen the way of life, but we find that our love easily fades. Keep speaking to us. Let us hear Your voice anew, and we will choose again to obey You. Let us sense the touch of Your hand, and we will cling to You. Steady our wobbly affections so that our love for You will increase throughout our days.

*No servant can serve two masters;
for either he will hate the one
and love the other,
or else he will be devoted to one
and despise the other.
You cannot serve God and wealth.*
— Luke 16:13

Help us, Lord Jesus! Our possessions so easily master us. We have seen how worldly pleasures fragment our lives and become cruel taskmasters. We need more than flimsy resolve to resist the seductive powers of this age. Expose our lesser affections as vain and worthless. Fortify our resolve to despise the treasures of this world. Yes, we love You, but call forth even greater love by the power of Your Spirit; a love that serves You with single-hearted joy. *Pray:*

- For struggling believers to set aside competing ambitions in order to serve Christ with authentic love.
- For those far from Christ to be nauseated by worldly enticements and become hungry for a life of serving God.

Seek God on behalf of Educators

That teachers and mentors will impart godly wisdom to help form character in their students; for needed tools and proper facilities; for those who home-school their children; for renewed zeal for truth and virtue; that they would have opportunity to know God in Christ; that believers would know how to pray for their students.

PRAYERWALK: As you walk around a school, pray for teachers, administrators and other staff.

...but everyone who is fully trained will be like his teacher.
— Luke 6:40 (NIV)

Seek God on behalf of the Americas and the Caribbean
Puerto Rico, Saint Kitts and Nevis, Saint Lucia, Saint Pierre and Miquelon

SEEK GOD
...for God to unite His people

Day 10
FRIDAY
FEBRUARY 19

*How good and pleasant it is
   when brothers live together in unity!...
For there the LORD bestows His blessing,
   even life forevermore.*
— Psalm 133:1, 3 (NIV)

We have been created and saved to unite in worship before You. There are times when we have worshiped together, tasting the joy of finally coming home as Your beloved daughters and sons. But we come to You now as a broken household. Minor differences have sometimes shattered friendships in the family of faith. At times we have ignored, despised or offended one another. Bring us together again. Train us in what is good. Restore what is pleasant. And bring to life the mighty blessing of being together as Your children.

*The glory which You have given Me
   I have given to them,
      that they may be one...
   so that the world may know
      that You sent Me, and loved them,
      even as You have loved Me.*
— John 17:22-23

When we are divided by petty agendas or grudges, we are rightly ridiculed by the world for our foolish religious superiority. But when we are fused as one in Your purpose, co-working with You as You co-worked with the Father, we can reflect Your glory to all the world. You have loved us and saved us so that we may bear Your beauty. Make us one so that the world will know the glorious love of the Father. *Pray:*

- For believers to set aside foolish jealousies, repent of sins against each other and be restored to vital unity.
- For divided congregations to become reconciled, reflecting Christ's beauty.
- For churches in your city to work and worship together.

Seek God on behalf of **Health Care Workers**

That God will equip health care workers of every kind to serve others with loving hearts; that God will bless them with perseverance and joy; that the pressure of their professions will not crush their families and friendships; that many will follow Christ.

PRAYERWALK: Pray on or near the grounds of a hospital or clinic.

Blessed is he who has regard for the weak; the LORD delivers him in times of trouble. The LORD will protect him and preserve his life; He will bless him in the land.
— Psalm 41:1-2 (NIV)

Seek God on behalf of **the Americas and the Caribbean**
Saint Vincent and the Grenadines, Suriname, Trinidad and Tobago, Turks and Caicos Islands

SEEK GOD
...to bring life from His people to the world

Day 11
SATURDAY
FEBRUARY 20

*So everything will live
  where the river goes...
By the river on its bank...will grow
  all kinds of trees for food.
Their leaves will not wither
  and their fruit will not fail...
  and their fruit will be for food
  and their leaves for healing.*
– Ezekiel 47:9, 12

You are sending a life-giving river to the world. Your life is already streaming from Your throne, releasing reviving power to us, and then through us to many more. Although the river may only be ankle deep at this hour, we anticipate days of grace when nothing will hold back the fullness of Your life from any place on earth. Unleash this river. Let it flow further than ever before. Remove whatever hinders Your goodness. Flood the nations that have not yet known Your boundless transforming love. Establish Your people everywhere, as if they were healing, nourishing trees amidst the nations.

*Now on the last day,
  the great day of the feast,
Jesus stood and cried out, saying,
  "If anyone is thirsty,
  let him come to Me and drink.
  He who believes in Me,
  as the Scripture said,
  'From his innermost being
  will flow rivers of living water.'"*
– John 7:37-38

Stand again in our midst, as You did in that day so long ago. Cry out again, raising Your voice so that multitudes will hear. Call us to come to drink deeply of You. Satisfy our deepest yearnings. Fill us to overflowing so that we become life-giving streams to many others.
Pray:

- That spiritually thirsty people will hear the voice of Christ calling them to Himself.
- For churches to become sources of healing for what is broken in our cities.
- For Christians to become conduits of God's life to others.

Seek God on behalf of **Ministries**

That Christian ministries will be founded on God's truth, anointed by God's power and funded by God's people; for refreshed encouragement upon those who labor in specialized service designed to increase the impact of local churches.

PRAYERWALK: Find a high point from which you can see much of the community. Pray that God would send needed Christian workers to your city and at the same time send Christian workers from your city.

Finally, brothers, pray for us that the word of the Lord will spread rapidly and be glorified, just as it did also with you.
– 2 Thessalonians 3:1

Seek God on behalf of **the Americas** and the **Caribbean**
United States of America, Uruguay, Venezuela, Virgin Islands of the USA

Seeking His **Light** to **Awaken** the Lost

FEBRUARY 21 - 27   WEEK 2

This week we will focus our attention on those who have yet to follow Christ. We will be asking God to awaken people from spiritual death. Persuasive words or demonstrations of kindness are not enough to cause people to turn toward God. If people ever come to follow Christ, it is because He draws them to Himself by bringing His light into their darkness.

People are not "lost" to God because they are misdirected or mixed up about religious things. God considers people to be lost when their relationship with Him is broken. That's why He loves to hear prayer on their behalf–so that His love will be revealed. Pray in hope that there will be great awakenings to Christ, the Light of the world.

Asia and the Pacific

This week we will extend our prayers for the peoples, cities, churches and families of Asia and the Pacific region.

SEEK GOD
...for God's light to bring abundant life

Day 12
SUNDAY
FEBRUARY 21

*How precious
 is Your lovingkindness, O God!
And the children of men take refuge
 in the shadow of Your wings.
They drink their fill of the abundance
 of Your house;
and You give them to drink of the river
 of Your delights.
For with You is the fountain of life.
In Your light we see light.*
— Psalm 36:7-9

From Your house there flows a river, a stream of steady love. Give our friends a taste of that love. Many keep themselves far from You. They are sure that You are angry with them, despising and punishing them. So they wander in the shadows where they think You cannot find them. Allow them to experience Your joy—the joy of Your heart when Your children simply love You. If You give them even a small sip of the fountain of Your favor, they will be drawn near to drink their fill. Overshadow them with the warmth of Your love and bring them all the way home.

*Then Jesus again spoke to them,
 saying,
 "I am the Light of the world.
 The one who follows Me
 will not walk in the darkness,
 but will have the Light of life."*
— John 8:12

Jesus, light of the world, give our friends who walk in darkness more than a momentary glimpse of Your life-changing light. Call them to follow You. By walking with You, Your light will reach inside them with healing and transforming power. Your light will give them life. *Pray:*

- For people to experience Christ as life-giving light, exposing darkness and imparting wisdom to live like Him.
- For the light of the gospel to bring many people alive in Christ.

Seek God on behalf of **the Poor**

For God to establish the poor so that their spiritual and physical needs are met with dignity and stability; that God will release them from cycles of oppression and despair; that God will reverse every curse and multiply blessing.

PRAYERWALK: Walk places of poverty and neglect. Ask the Holy Spirit to give you His eyes and His heart in order to pray from hope, not pity. What grieves or gladdens God as He walks amidst the poor?

I know that the LORD will maintain the cause of the afflicted and justice for the poor.
— Psalm 140:12

Seek God on behalf of **Asia and the Pacific**
Afghanistan, American Samoa, Antarctica, Australia, Bangladesh, Bhutan, Brunei, Cambodia

SEEK GOD
...to open the eyes of the blind

Day 13
MONDAY
FEBRUARY 22

*How blessed is the one
whose help is the God of Jacob,
whose hope is in the LORD his God...
The LORD sets the prisoners free.
The LORD opens the eyes of the blind.
The LORD raises up those
who are bowed down.*
— Psalm 146:5, 8

You have long been our help and our hope. Since the days of Abraham, Isaac and Jacob You have promised blessing upon Your people. In Jesus that hope of blessing is confirmed. We are blessed in Him, and so we ask for Your blessing to come upon the spiritually blind and broken of our city. They may not consider themselves to be blind. They may not have known to call upon You for help. And so we pray on their behalf: Open the doors of spiritual bondage. Lift those who have been crumpled by sorrow. Open their eyes to see the beauty of Christ and the hope of trusting Him.

*Jesus...said, "What do you want Me
to do for you?" They said to Him,
"Lord, we want our eyes to be opened."
Moved with compassion, Jesus touched
their eyes; and immediately they
regained their sight and followed Him.*
— Matthew 20:32-34

How would our friends answer if You asked them what they wanted from You? They may not know what they truly desire. Keep searching their souls. Find those who are desperate to have their vision restored. Move in Your immense compassion, gently touching them so that their eyes are open to You. Restore the spiritual sight of many throughout our city. Those who see You will follow You. *Pray:*

- For the eyes of the spiritually blind to be opened to recognize God's love.
- That people would experience the amazing compassion of Jesus.
- For people who encounter Christ to follow Him faithfully.

Seek God on behalf of **Refugees**

For safe, legal immigration and for conditions to improve in homelands so that extended families will be united; for Christians to open homes and hearts to them; for the gospel to be conveyed clearly; for those desiring to return to homelands to be granted asylum and repatriation; that God would open the way for those desiring a new home to be resettled.

PRAYERWALK: Pray prayers of welcome, protection and blessing for refugees and immigrants in your community.

He defends the cause of the fatherless and the widow, and loves the alien, giving him food and clothing. And you are to love those who are aliens, for you yourselves were aliens in Egypt.
– Deuteronomy 10:18-19 (NIV)

Seek God on behalf of **Asia and the Pacific**

China-People's Republic, China-Taiwan, Christmas Island, Cocos (Keeling) Islands, Cook Islands, Fiji

SEEK GOD
...for God to prevail over powers of darkness

Day 14
TUESDAY
FEBRUARY 23

The LORD will go forth like a warrior, He will arouse His zeal like a man of war. He will utter a shout, yes, He will raise a war cry. He will prevail against His enemies. ..."I will lead the blind
  by a way they do not know.
  In paths they do not know
  I will guide them.
  I will make darkness
  into light before them."
— Isaiah 42:13, 16

Come on, awesome God. You have heard our cry for help. In Your mercy and in Your might, arouse Yourself as our champion warrior. Raise Your voice as a shout of war denouncing the spiritual powers that still hold millions captive in our land. Lift Your voice again, but as a tender shepherd, to summon those who are oppressed or lost. Lead many to freedom, like a herdsman bringing his flock homeward. Fight this war in ways that we cannot. Lead us in ways of freedom that we will never discover on our own. Prevail over evil so decisively that our darkness is turned to Your light.

Now judgment is upon this world; now the ruler of this world will be cast out. And I, if I am lifted up from the earth, will draw all men to Myself...While you have the Light, believe in the Light, so that you may become sons of Light.
— John 12:31-32, 36

Lord Jesus, Your suffering on the cross has broken and shamed every satanic power. You are now raised from death and exalted in resurrection life over all the earth. You did not die to merely conquer the evil one, but to bring people back into full relationship with You. Fulfill that great purpose in our day. Lift the light of Your glory among the people of our city. Be honored by the praise of Your people. Be exalted by the telling of the gospel. Cause many to come to You and become children of light who reflect Your glory. *Pray:*

- For God to deliver those afflicted by demonic powers in your city.
- For those trapped in cults or the occult, that the Lord would liberate them from darkness to walk in light.

Seek God on behalf of **Pastors**

That pastors and church leaders will be filled with wisdom; that they will be honored by those they serve; that God will pour His Spirit upon them in power and humility, giving fresh intimacy with Jesus; for protection from the plots of the evil one against their families; that deep friendships with other pastors will grow.

PRAYERWALK: Pray outside a church building for the pastor(s) who serve(s) that church.

Be shepherds of God's flock that is under your care...Cast all your anxiety on Him because He cares for you.
— 1 Peter 5:2, 7 (NIV)

Seek God on behalf of **Asia and the Pacific**

French Polynesia, Guam, Hong Kong, India, Indonesia, Japan, Kiribati

SEEK GOD
...to rescue people from spiritual darkness

Day 15
WEDNESDAY
FEBRUARY 24

*There were those who dwelt in darkness
  and in the shadow of death,
prisoners in misery and chains,
  because they had rebelled
  against the words of God...
Then they cried out to the LORD
  in their trouble.
He saved them...
He brought them out of darkness
  and the shadow of death
  and broke their bands apart.*
— Psalm 107:10-11, 13-14

Many are locked in lifestyles that hold them in darkness. Some search in vain for escape from the grim misery of their lives. Some feel the chill of death already overshadowing them. Hear their cry, O God. Penetrate prisons locked by pride. Shatter the habits that bind them like chains. Break the bars of resentment and hatred that keep them from authentic relationships of love. Light up the darkness of their lives so they can walk away from the grief of sin and follow You.

*Men loved the darkness rather than
  the Light, for their deeds were evil...
But he who practices the truth
comes to the Light,
  so that his deeds may be manifested
  as having been wrought in God.*
— John 3:19, 21

You constantly bring the light of Your love into many people's lives. But again and again, they choose to love darkness, preferring to hide in the shadows of habitual sin. We pray that You would energize them by the great power of Your grace to take even one step toward the light of Your truth. And after that first step, give them another, and then another, until they find themselves drawn into the bright hope that they shall be changed. *Pray:*

- For God to subdue powers of evil that hold people in darkness.
- For the light of the gospel to expose the bondage of rebellion, and to illumine the hope of freedom in Jesus.
- For new believers to put truth into daily practice.

Seek God on behalf of **Prisoners and their Families**

That people in jails and prisons will hear the gospel and follow Christ; for fellowships of believers to multiply; that they be protected from violence and forces of spiritual evil; that the spouses and children of prisoners would be sustained, protected, provided for and honored rightly; that released prisoners find strength and wisdom to live abundant lives.

*You who seek God,
let your heart revive.
For the LORD hears
the needy, and does
not despise His who
are prisoners.*
— Psalm 69:32-33

PRAYERWALK: Pray near a jail or correctional facility. Or pray for homes in your neighborhood that may have family members or loved ones in prison.

Seek God on behalf of **Asia and the Pacific**
Korea-North, Korea-South, Laos, Macau, Malaysia, Maldives, Marshall Islands, Micronesia

SEEK GOD
...for the word of God to be understood

Day 16
THURSDAY
FEBRUARY 25

The unfolding of Your words gives light. It gives understanding to the simple.
— Psalm 119:130

We long for Your words to become alive in the hearts of our friends. In fear, pride or folly, some of them have darkened the windows of their lives. Even if they have heard the words before, we ask You to send Your word to them yet again. Give them humility of heart to listen and hear Your voice. Send word-bearers who are humble and wise, whose lives match the message. Even a small portion of Your word, when unfolded faithfully, can burst into radiant light. And with Your light bring life.

Then He opened their minds to understand the Scriptures.
— Luke 24:45

Lord Jesus, when You unrolled the scrolls in synagogues, You surprised the crowds by opening the Scriptures like no one else had ever done. But You did more than merely open the words, You opened the minds of Your followers to understand. Unblock the minds of those who hear Your word today. Pour light upon the pages as they read. Clear away deception so they will comprehend the amazing greatness of what You have done. *Pray:*

- For people to read the Bible together, understanding what they read, and obeying what they understand.
- For the Scriptures to get into the hands of truth-seekers in your city.
- That the Spirit of God would illumine His word, bringing clarity and conviction.

Seek God on behalf of **University Students**

Pray for many students to follow Christ; for the truth to radiate in a setting that is often hostile and cynical toward matters of faith; for students to make wise decisions, to form godly lifestyles and to shape their careers and ambitions to fulfill God's global purposes. Pray for leadership to be strong among Christian groups on campuses; for the advance of movements of prayer and mission mobilization; for the ministries that focus on students.

PRAYERWALK: Pray for students at a place of higher education.

Since my youth, O God, you have taught me, and to this day I declare your marvelous deeds.
— Psalm 71:17 (NIV)

Seek God on behalf of **Asia and the Pacific**
Mongolia, Myanmar, Nauru, Nepal, New Caledonia, New Zealand, Niue, Norfolk Island

SEEK GOD
...for revelation leading to repentance

Day 17
FRIDAY
FEBRUARY 26

*I have heard of You
   by the hearing of the ear;
but now my eye sees You.
Therefore I retract,
   and I repent in dust and ashes.*
— Job 42:5-6

We pray for the ones who have heard about You, and yet they remain stone-cold to You. Some have been told that You are the source of their suffering. Others are disappointed that You have failed to give them quick solutions to their problems. Reveal Yourself in all Your majesty. Vindicate Your reputation by disclosing Your mighty mercy. Allow them to see how their sin has brought incredible sorrow to Your heart. Disclose Your awesome kindness, so that their stony hearts melt in view of how determined You are to love them. Cause them to behold Jesus Himself—in all His excellence and humility. Receive them with joy as they turn to You.

*"Who is He, Lord,
   that I may believe in Him?"
Jesus said to him,
   "You have both seen Him, and
   He is the one who is talking with you."
And he said, "Lord, I believe."
And he worshiped Him.*
— John 9:36-38

Some of our friends seem cynical or blind to You. But perhaps they would trust You if they came to know who You really are. Make Yourself known to them as You have revealed Yourself to millions of others. Show them that You are the same Jesus who acted in the Gospels with eye-opening power. May the spiritually blind come to see. May those who see come to believe. And may those who believe become dedicated worshipers.
Pray:

- For the hard-hearted to encounter Christ's love so clearly that they reject false ideas about God.

- For spiritually blind people to see Jesus Christ so that they trust Him and become full-hearted worshipers.

Seek God on behalf of **Physically Disabled People**

That they will be surrounded with loving friends and family; for steady refreshment of their hearts toward God; for physical stamina and healing; for endurance through chronic pain; for financial provision to cover the cost of therapy and special care; that they will know and display the love of God.

PRAYERWALK: Pray along the same route that a person with disabilities might use to move through your neighborhood, school or workplace. As you do, pray for someone you know with disabilities.

In all their affliction He was afflicted... In His love and in His mercy He redeemed them, and He lifted them and carried them all the days of old. — Isaiah 63:9

Seek God on behalf of **Asia and the Pacific**
Northern Mariana Islands, Pakistan, Palau, Papua New Guinea, Philippines, Samoa, Singapore, Solomon Islands

SEEK GOD
...for the light of the gospel to shine

Day 18
SATURDAY
FEBRUARY 27

*The people who walk in darkness
    will see a great light.
Those who live in a dark land,
    the light will shine on them.*
— Isaiah 9:2

We know the anguish of living in the darkness of our hearts, stumbling over our fears, as if it were always night. Lord of light, we plead for our friends who shuffle along through their days, groping with uncertainty, as if they were blind. They have every good intention, but they cannot find their way. Bring light from heaven upon them, as You did for us. There is no way we can throw on a switch for them. There is no candle we can light. Lift the veil of darkness. Shine like the sun upon their hearts so that they follow You with joy.

*Because of the tender mercy of our God,
    with which the Sunrise
    from on high will visit us,
to shine upon those who sit in darkness
    and the shadow of death.*
— Luke 1:78-79

You have promised to come like the dawn, slow and steady, but eventually brightening everything. When You came, Lord Jesus, You came like a sunrise, shedding life-giving light on those who were captive to a heavy spiritual darkness. Many could suddenly see. And they began to seek You. We ask You now for such an outpouring of Your light upon our city. Come upon the people of our community, surprising them with a different kind of dawn—coming not from the east, but instead, coming from above—revealing the tender power of Your love. *Pray:*

- For Christ's light to shine into the darkened hearts of people you know.
- For God to visit your community, revealing His mercy to many.

Seek God on behalf of **Mothers**

That God will powerfully refresh mothers in the honor and glory of motherhood; that they will be strengthened with grace, wisdom and love in serving their children; that they will be loved, protected and served by committed husbands; that mothers will model and express God's own nurturing love.

PRAYERWALK: Walk through your neighborhood, praying for mothers and grandmothers.

She is clothed with strength and dignity; she can laugh at the days to come. She speaks with wisdom... Her children arise and call her blessed; her husband also, and he praises her.
— Proverbs 31:25-26, 28 (NIV)

Seek God on behalf of **Asia and the Pacific**
Sri Lanka, Thailand, Tibet, Timor Leste, Tonga, Tuvalu, Vanuatu, Vietnam, Wallis and Futuna

Seeking His **Glory** in **Evangelizing** All Peoples

FEBRUARY 28 - MARCH 5   WEEK 3

As God works by the power of the gospel, people are transformed by Christ. Their families and communities begin to change, and God is increasingly thanked for His goodness. God receives more glory as people grow into the image of Christ and offer God explicit worship by His Spirit.

This week we are praying for every people group to be evangelized. We aren't overreaching as we focus on the glory Christ will gain for the Father in a thoroughly evangelized world. Such hope is clearly promised in Scripture. God has been moving in tremendous ways in many parts of the world. Now is the time to pray that God will move even more powerfully so that He will be glorified by a movement of loving obedience in every people throughout the communities of the world.

Africa

This week we will be praying for the cities, peoples, tribes and countries of the continent of Africa.

SEEK GOD
...for His renown among all peoples

Day 19
SUNDAY
FEBRUARY 28

Give thanks to the LORD, call on His name.
Make known His deeds among the peoples.
Make them remember
   that His name is exalted...
   He has done excellent things.
Let this be known throughout the earth.
— Isaiah 12:4-5

Living God, although You are heartily praised in our churches, You are lightly regarded, fiercely hated, or utterly ignored by many in our city. For too long You have gone anonymous. People do not recognize the good things that You constantly do for them. Your goodness is deemed to be luck or coincidence. Kindness is considered a random thing. Lord of glory, we ask You to do something great for Your name. Become famous for who You really are. Re-establish Your reputation among those who have forgotten You. Stir Your people to tell the story of Your glory in their lives so that You are praised beyond the walls of our churches.

When you pray, say: "Father, hallowed be Your name." — Luke 11:2

Jesus, You were jealous for Your Father's glory. Everything You did, said and prayed was intended to reveal the singular beauty of the Father's heart. Show us how to pray for His renown. Bolster our courage so that we pray large enough to match the great things that the Father longs to do in our community. May the marvels of the Father's life and blessing soon become known and celebrated among those who have never experienced His love. *Pray:*

- For believers to become story-tellers, recounting to friends and neighbors what God has done for them.
- That God will reveal Himself to people who have denied or defied Him.
- For God to be thanked for doing good things in your community.

Seek God on behalf of **Government Leaders**

That they will be examples of righteousness to our society; that they will experience God's wisdom in their deliberations; that they will speak and carry out dealings with truth; that they will not hinder the service and worship of Jesus Christ; that they will come to know, honor and follow Christ.

PRAYERWALK: Visit a center of city, county, state or federal government. Pray on or near the site. Leave a short note for a particular official which describes your prayers for God to bless him or her.

I urge, then, first of all, that requests, prayers, intercession and thanksgiving be made for everyone — for kings and all those in authority.
– 1 Timothy 2:1-2 (NIV)

Seek God on behalf of **Africa**
Angola, Benin, Botswana, Burkina Faso, Burundi, Cameroon, Cape Verde Islands

SEEK GOD
...that His people would reflect His great name

Day 20
MONDAY
FEBRUARY 29

*Do something for the sake of Your name.
   For our backsliding is great;
   we have sinned against You...
Why are You like a stranger in the land,
   like a traveler who stays only a night?
Why are You like a man taken by surprise,
   like a warrior powerless to save?
You are among us, O LORD,
   and we bear Your name!
Do not forsake us!*
                 – Jeremiah 14:7-9 (NIV)

Our sin has degraded Your reputation. We are ashamed to admit that we have sometimes dishonored Your name. When we backslide, in doubt or self-reliance, onlooking unbelievers conclude that You are not to be trusted. They regard You as aloof, uncaring or even cruel. And so You have become a bygone memory, a phantom of the ancient past. Forgive us for failing to glorify You. We beg You to vindicate Your name. You are wise, mighty and good. Become great again in our sight. Be exalted in our city and glorious among the nations.

*"Father, glorify Your name."
Then a voice came out of heaven:
   "I have both glorified it,
   and will glorify it again."*
                 – John 12:28

Our Father, we echo this, the prayer of Your Son, that in these days, Your renown would be greater than ever. You greatly glorified Yourself in Jesus. Now, as You have promised, glorify Your name yet again. If You are known truly, then You can be followed fully. Father, glorify Your name! *Pray:*

- For backslidden Christians to become faithful, God-honoring followers of Christ.
- For God to be glorified in the words, deeds and prayers of His people.

Seek God on behalf of **News Media**

For people throughout the industries of broadcast and print media to come to know Jesus personally; that attitudes of cynicism will be changed; for those who love Christ to be strengthened in wisdom; for a growing emphasis in their work on that which carries virtue and conveys the values of Christ's kingdom throughout the city.

PRAYERWALK: Visit a media center, a broadcast station or a publisher of print media. Pray for some who are associated with that particular enterprise.

These are the things which you should do: speak the truth to one another; judge with truth and judgment for peace in your gates.
      – Zechariah 8:16

Seek God on behalf of **Africa**

Central African Republic, Chad, Comoros,
Congo-Democratic Republic (Zaire), Cote d'Ivoire, Djibouti

SEEK GOD
...to display His love and power by answered prayer

Day 21
TUESDAY
MARCH 1

*Hear in heaven Your dwelling place,
  and do according to all
   for which the foreigner calls to You,
in order that all the peoples of the earth
  may know Your name,
  to fear You, as do Your people.*
— 1 Kings 8:43

Hear and answer lost people when they pray so that You will be glorified in their sight. No matter how stubbornly they may have fought You, regardless of how far they may have fled from You, have mercy and hear their cry. Hear their desperation with Your perfect wisdom. Be moved by their sorrows with Your boundless compassion. Act swiftly, responding to the weakest whisper of prayer. Demonstrate Your power, win their praise and call them to Your kingdom.

*They were all struck with astonishment
  and began glorifying God;
  and they were filled with fear, saying,
"We have seen remarkable things today."*
— Luke 5:26

Lord Jesus, You responded with compassion to the faith of ordinary people as they brought their friends and family members to You. God worked in response to Your prayer with such astounding power that reports rippled throughout entire communities. Honor again the faith of ordinary people who cry out to You. Demonstrate the loving power of the living God so decisively that many will openly exclaim Your praise. *Pray:*

- For God to hear and to answer the prayers of people who do not yet know Christ.
- For Christians to pray for others in wise and sensitive ways.

Seek God on behalf of **Orphans**

Pray for children who have lost their parents, or who are now in foster care away from their birth parents; for safe, loving, permanent homes with godly adoptive or foster parents; for healing from any effects of physical, emotional or sexual abuse; for siblings to be adopted together; for thousands of young people who have already "aged out" of adoptive services, that they will find wise mentors and a secure place in the family of God.

PRAYERWALK: In many neighborhoods God is calling people to become foster or adoptive parents. Pray that they act in His grace, love and wisdom.

You have heard the desire of the humble. You will strengthen their heart. You will incline Your ear to vindicate the orphan and the oppressed.
– Psalm 10:17-18

Seek God on behalf of **Africa**

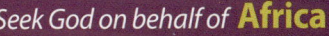

Equatorial Guinea, Eritrea, Ethiopia, Gabon, Gambia, Ghana, Guinea, Guinea Bissau

SEEK GOD
...to be recognized and honored by leaders

Day 22
WEDNESDAY
MARCH 2

O kings, show discernment;
  take warning, O judges of the earth.
Worship the LORD with reverence
  and rejoice with trembling...
    How blessed are all
    who take refuge in Him!
        – Psalm 2:10-12

We pray for the leaders of our land. The same forces that exalted them to power could just as quickly turn on them. But angry voters and hostile armies are not their greatest danger. They stand before You, Almighty God, accountable for all their deeds. Because they govern Your little ones and make decisions concerning justice, they will answer to You for every choice and each word. And so we pray that they will submit their governance to Your greater wisdom. Give them hope in Your majesty as Judge of all the earth. May they come to honor You openly. Protect and encourage them as they find true refuge in You. Bless the cities and lands they serve so that You are known by all and exalted by many.

"When you have found Him, report to me,
  so that I too may come and worship Him."
After hearing the king,
  they went their way...
When they saw the star,
  they rejoiced exceedingly with great joy.
After coming into the house...
  they fell to the ground and worshiped Him.
        – Matthew 2:8-11

Lord Jesus, move upon our leaders so that they will give You glory. Governing leaders are still drawn to You for all the reasons they searched for You at Your birth. Some are threatened by Your coming kingship and so try to oppose You, as if they could rival Your majesty. Yet others wisely rejoice to welcome Your coming kingdom. Reveal Yourself so that leaders honor You as the only one worthy of worship in all the earth. *Pray:*

- For local, state and national officials to know the truth of Christ and His kingdom.
- For government leaders who do fear God to find courage to openly express reverence and honor for Jesus Christ.

Seek God on behalf of **Business People**

Ask God to bless those who base business practices in righteousness. Pray that God will prosper those who pursue their business as mission for God's kingdom. Pray for the gospel to spread in the marketplace; for righteous managers and executives; for creative, godly entrepreneurs. Pray that God would frustrate plans which escalate injustice.

PRAYERWALK: As you pass through a place of business today, pray for Christ to be followed and for His name to be honored in that setting. Pray for God to bless the endeavors that exemplify His kingdom.

But remember the LORD your God, for it is He who gives you the ability to produce wealth.
– Deuteronomy 8:18 (NIV)

Seek God on behalf of **Africa**

Kenya, Lesotho, Liberia, Madagascar, Malawi, Mali, Mauritania, Mauritius

SEEK GOD
...for every people group to hear the gospel

Day 23
THURSDAY
MARCH 3

*Sing to the LORD, all the earth.
Proclaim good tidings
    of His salvation from day to day.
Tell of His glory among the nations,
His wonderful deeds
    among all the peoples...
And let them say among the nations,
    "The LORD reigns."*
– 1 Chronicles 16:23-24

May the word of Your coming kingdom be announced with such winsome clarity that all the peoples of the earth will hear of Your salvation. You have brought people from distant nations to the cities of our land, but many are still far from You. Send Your word out like a song, so that the sweet reality of Your love seeps into the souls of those who hear. May Your love be told as an epic story so that people are amazed by the beauty of what You have done for them. Let Your story be told again and again, until every people on earth and every group of our city has heard the story of Your glory.

*"Return to your house and describe
    what great things God has done for you."
    So he went away,
proclaiming throughout the whole city
    what great things
        Jesus had done for him.*
– Luke 8:39

One man reported the things You did for him to his own family. Then the news went beyond his household so that the whole city heard. Do the same thing yet again in our city. May one relay the gospel to another, and then throughout their households. Make Your word resound through neighborhoods and networks of friends. Fill our entire community with fresh tellings of the gospel. And from our city, send the message to many peoples and places across the face of the earth. *Pray:*

- For believers to tell their families the story of what Jesus has done for them.
- For the glory and greatness of the gospel to be conveyed in heart-stirring music.
- For gospel movements to surge throughout whole cities.

Seek God on behalf of **Men**

That men will seek God and honor Him in faithfulness, wisdom and truth; for their identity to be centered in Christ-like servant leadership; that the vision of their lives would be to serve and advance God's purposes.

PRAYERWALK: Ask God to help you focus prayers of blessing on a few of the men that you see today.

Let not the wise man boast of his wisdom or the strong man boast of his strength or the rich man boast of his riches, but let him who boasts boast about this: that he understands and knows Me.
– Jeremiah 9:23-24 (NIV)

Seek God on behalf of **Africa**
Mayotte, Mozambique, Namibia, Niger, Nigeria, Republic of Congo, Réunion

SEEK GOD
...that many would know and follow Him

Day 24
FRIDAY
MARCH 4

*Many peoples and the inhabitants
of many cities will yet come,
and the inhabitants of one city
will go to another and say,
"Let us go at once to entreat the LORD
and seek the LORD Almighty.
I myself am going."
And many peoples
and powerful nations will come.*
— Zechariah 8:20-22 (NIV)

We praise You for the great movements to Christ in far-off places of the earth. Chain reactions of faith are drawing many thousands to You every day. First a family, then a clan and then many throughout entire peoples suddenly surge toward Christ. Yet we can be satisfied if only a few visitors come to our Sunday morning worship. But since Your promise is greater, our hearts know better. Revivals will restore Your wayward people, but we ask You to fulfill Your promise for great awakenings to draw many and mighty nations to seek You. Make our city the scene of such escalating movements.

*The Pharisees said to one another...
"Look how the whole world
has gone after Him!"*
— John 12:19 (NIV)

Lord Jesus, even Your enemies felt that the whole world was coming to You. Great throngs sought You in the cities. Crowds found You in the countryside. Leaders came to You in secret. In our day, and in our community, we ask that You would call forth movements of inquiry, repentance and faith. Train faithful followers to become fruitful leaders who will draw even more to seek You.
Pray:

- For the Spirit of God to ignite the hearts of many to seek and to know Jesus.
- For God to raise up disciple-making men and women to sustain new Christward movements.

Seek God on behalf of **Native Peoples**

For native peoples who live in or near your city to be honored for who they are and for all God intends them to be; that God would heal the wounds to our nation that have resulted from broken treaties and mistreatment; that the tribes will be treated justly and find their destiny and highest dignity; that churches will flourish among them and that God's praise will resound in native languages.

PRAYERWALK: As you prayerwalk, consider the native peoples who first dwelt in the area that has become your city. Pray for their descendants.

*I will set My justice
for a light of the
peoples.*
— Isaiah 51:4

Seek God on behalf of **Africa**

Rwanda, Saint Helena, Sao Tome and Principe, Senegal, Seychelles, Sierra Leone, Somalia, South Africa

SEEK GOD
...for God to be worshiped by all peoples

Day 25
SATURDAY
MARCH 5

*All nations whom You have made
shall come and worship
before You, O Lord,
and they shall glorify Your name.
For You are great
and do wondrous deeds.
You alone are God.* — Psalm 86:9-10

You have set Your heart to call forth a worshiping people from every language and land. You have made them, and by the blood and life of Christ You have re-made them, some from every people. The coming extravaganza of worshipers is more certain than today's headlines. And so we pray with confidence: Complete what You have begun! Surpass Yourself by exhibiting even greater deeds of healing and power. Become famous for transforming lives. Gather worshipers from the diverse peoples in our city. Be honored as the only living God. And may Your praise resound in all the earth.

*But an hour is coming, and now is,
when the true worshipers will worship
the Father in spirit and truth;
for such people the Father seeks
to be His worshipers.* — John 4:23

We do not have to persuade You to seek worshipers. You have yearned to be worshiped with a passion that is ancient, vast and forceful, beyond human description. It is right for us to plead that Your love would be answered by love-filled worship from all peoples. Now is the hour. Search our city and find the devoted worshipers You have so long desired. *Pray:*

- For worship leaders to be filled with God's Spirit and focused on biblical truth.
- For Christians to find themselves energized by the Father's zeal to be truly worshiped in love.
- For Christ-centered worship to emerge in every ethnic community of your city.

Seek God on behalf of **Judges** and **Law Enforcement**

Pray for wisdom, principled patience and gentle authority; for physical and emotional protection; for strength and blessing for their families; that they will become agents of God's hand to resist evil and bring an environment in which heaven's justice can increase.

PRAYERWALK: Pray outside the nearest police station or court. Leave a short personal note for judges or police leaders letting them know how Christians are praying for them today.

Blessed are they who maintain justice, who constantly do what is right.
— Psalm 106:3 (NIV)

Seek God on behalf of **Africa**

South Sudan, Sudan, Swaziland, Tanzania, Togo, Uganda, Western Sahara, Zambia, Zimbabwe

Seeking His **Righteousness** in Our **Communities**

MARCH 6-12 WEEK 4

Righteousness is sometimes misunderstood as merely being right. But righteousness has nothing to do with religious superiority. It is simply life rightly lived in God's sight. Because of Christ's life and power, broken people can be changed to live in Christ's righteousness.

God has purposed to bring about much more than personal righteousness. The kingdom of God is marked by peace, joy and righteousness lived out in everyday life (Romans 14:17). God desires to change many people at once so that the righteous character of Christ goes on display throughout entire communities.

Europe and **Central Asia**

This fourth week we will direct our prayers with and for the people, churches and countries of Europe and Central Asia.

SEEK GOD
...for the righteousness of a few to bring blessing on many

Day 26
SUNDAY
MARCH 6

*Abraham will surely become a great...
nation, and in him all the nations
of the earth will be blessed...
For I have chosen him so that he may
command his children and his household
after him to keep the way of the LORD
by doing righteousness and justice,
so that the LORD may bring upon Abraham
what He has spoken about him.*
– Genesis 18:18-19

As Abraham prayed for the city of Sodom, You disclosed Your ways to him: Because of the righteousness of a few, You would show mercy and blessing on many. We approach You now as Abraham's children by faith, that You would have mercy and bring blessing on our community. We cannot claim to have fully lived out the justice and righteousness of Christ. Do more than forgive us. Reform us and train us to be the righteous people that You have long desired. As You transform our lives in Christ's righteousness, even though we are few, bring about some of Your long-promised blessing upon many of our city.

*...for in this way it is fitting for us
to fulfill all righteousness.*
– Matthew 3:15

Lord Jesus, when You stepped forward to be baptized, You were not seeking to be made righteous. You had lived a perfect life and had no need to be washed clean. Instead, You were seeking to fulfill a larger purpose, that many would be transformed by Your life in order to live right lives. Fulfill what You began. Make many people righteous in the sight of God as they follow You in faith. May their lives become a spectacle of Your character, justice and truth in the sight of many of our city. *Pray:*

- That people will trust and follow Christ, and live right lives by His power.
- That justice would be pursued by Christians of your city.

Seek God on behalf of **Unemployed People**

That God will meet the needs of those without work in a way that they can clearly thank God for His provision; that they will soon find meaningful employment and glorify God for it; that God will open the way for righteous trade so that the entire city prospers in His provision.

PRAYERWALK: Pray for those in your neighborhood who have recently lost their job or are struggling to find one.

That everyone may eat and drink, and find satisfaction in all his toil–this is the gift of God.
– Ecclesiastes 3:13 (NIV)

Seek God on behalf of **Europe and Central Asia**

Albania, Andorra, Armenia, Austria, Azerbaijan, Belarus,
Belgium, Bosnia and Herzegovina, Bulgaria

SEEK GOD
...to intervene in order to bring forth justice

Day 27
MONDAY
MARCH 7

Arise, O LORD, in Your anger...
O let the evil of the wicked come to an end,
but establish the righteous.
For the righteous God
tries the hearts and minds...
God is a righteous judge, and
a God who has indignation every day.
— Psalm 7:6, 9, 11

Every day You behold the evil of those who exploit the weak, abuse the young or cheat the poor. And every single day You smolder with rage at the sight. Arise, O Judge of all the earth! We cry out for justice, not because we are righteous, but because You are righteous. Only in You is highest righteousness, and at the same time, utmost mercy. And so with awe and fear we approach You, knowing our brokenness. We call on You to restrain runaway evil. And at the same time, we ask You to redeem broken people to become like Your Son. Examine our hearts and reshape our minds, so that we love what is delightful in Your sight.

Will not God bring about justice
for His chosen ones,
who cry out to Him day and night?
Will He keep putting them off?
I tell you, He will see that they get justice,
and quickly. However, when the Son of Man
comes, will He find faith on the earth?
— Luke 18:7-8 (NIV)

We want to answer "Yes," to Your question. You will indeed find faith on the earth. May we be among those found praying for You to overturn the works of darkness. We now approach Your court to present our case, even if we must come daily to repeat the same appeal again and again. Overrule the evil that abuses many people of our land. Intervene to bring justice. When You return, we want to be among those who never gave up asking You to put Your justice on display within the days of history. *Pray:*

- For the laws of the land to be framed upon God's standards of righteousness.
- For God to overturn the status quo of injustice and entrenched evil.

Seek God on behalf of **Youth**

For teens to radically and completely commit their lives to Christ; to make wise choices; for older mentors; for authentic friendships with their peers who are following Jesus; for open trust and communication with parents; for God's intentions for their generation to come forth in fullest measure.

PRAYERWALK: Pray with your eyes open for people in their teens. Envision them following Christ five, ten or more years from now.

Then our sons in their youth will be like well-nurtured plants, and our daughters will be like pillars carved to adorn a palace... Blessed are the people whose God is the LORD!
— Psalm 144:12,15 (NIV)

Seek God on behalf of **Europe and Central Asia**

Canary Islands, Croatia, Czech Republic, Denmark, Estonia, Faeroe Islands, Finland

SEEK GOD
...to inspire a yearning for righteousness

Day 28
TUESDAY
MARCH 8

*While following the way of
Your judgments, O LORD,
we have waited for You eagerly.
Your name, even Your memory,
is the desire of our souls.
...Indeed, my spirit within me
seeks You diligently; for when the
earth experiences Your judgments
the inhabitants of the world
learn righteousness.* — Isaiah 26:8-9

In these drastic days Your dealings are as mysterious as they are magnificent. We watch and yearn in hope for You to vindicate Your good and great name. Though darkness appears to prevail, You will not fail to bring Your kingly rule upon the earth. We pray for those who pursue evil, heedless of Your love or Your judgment. Show them Your mercy! Reveal to them the excellence of Your wisdom and the beauty of Your righteousness. Awaken many to the great hope of Your coming, and may they come to welcome Your Lordship now.

*Blessed are those who hunger
and thirst for righteousness,
for they shall be satisfied.* — Matthew 5:6

Of course we like the idea of living righteously. It sounds proper and virtuous. But we may have treated true righteousness as if it were merely an option for the super-committed. But the beauty of Christ's righteousness is among Your greatest gifts. Ignite a deep and increasing desire for the risen, living Jesus to bring about His life in our midst. Cause this longing to be as all-consuming as hunger, and as powerful as thirst. Satisfy our hope to see the righteousness of God flourish in our city. *Pray:*

- For God to free people from hypnotic delusions of sin to experience the satisfying joy of life in Christ.
- For God to awaken in people a yearning like hunger to live in the fullness of Christ's righteousness.
- For transformed lives to bring about changed communities that reflect the light and love of Christ.

Seek God on behalf of **Substance Abusers**

That God will break every form of bondage, including alcoholism and drug addiction. Pray for wise counselors to bring intervention and help. Pray that God will heal the minds and bodies of substance abusers; that they will turn from self-centeredness to living their lives for Christ.

PRAYERWALK: Consider those in your neighborhood who may be bound by addiction to drugs or alcohol. Ask God to free them.

On the day the LORD gives you relief from suffering and turmoil and cruel bondage.
– Isaiah 14:3 (NIV)

Seek God on behalf of **Europe and Central Asia**
France, Georgia, Germany, Gibraltar, Greece, Hungary, Iceland, Ireland

SEEK GOD
...for His Spirit to empower His people

Day 29
WEDNESDAY
MARCH 9

The Spirit of the Lord GOD is upon me...
To proclaim the favorable year of the LORD.
...So they will be called oaks of righteousness, the planting of the LORD, that He may be glorified.
Then they will rebuild the ancient ruins. They will raise up the former devastations; and they will repair the ruined cities, the desolations of many generations.
— Isaiah 61:1-4

Send Your Spirit upon Your people. Plant seeds of hope in the hearts of the downcast. Cause them to grow quickly and spread widely, implanting righteousness where there was none. Raise up Your people to rebuild devastated communities, even places considered dead for generations. The remade city does not consist of steel beams or sleek glass. The city You are creating is alive and powerful with righteous life, renewed from within, growing slow and strong like a forest of solid oaks. Come upon us Spirit of God. Bring the promised time of favor for our city.

"The Spirit of the Lord is upon Me, because He anointed Me to preach the gospel to the poor. He has sent Me to proclaim release to the captives, and recovery of sight to the blind, to set free those who are oppressed, to proclaim the favorable year of the Lord."
...And He began to say to them, "Today this Scripture has been fulfilled in your hearing."
— Luke 4:18-19, 21

The Spirit of the Lord is still upon You, Anointed One. Because You live with resurrected power, the same "year of favor" continues to this day. Push this promise to even greater fulfillment in this hour. Pour Your Spirit upon all of Your people. Extend favor upon entire communities, giving many the opportunity to hear Your word, to see Your love and to be lifted from all that binds them. *Pray:*

- For God to empower Christians by His Spirit to renew their communities.
- For many to experience God's favor.

Seek God on behalf of **Depressed People**

That God's healing presence will reach them; that the light of truth will dispel lies and the oppressive power of Satan; for helpful counsel; for the healing of long-standing wounds of mind and soul; that they would know the comfort and joy of the Holy Spirit; for the renewing of their minds in Christ.

PRAYERWALK: Pray for people you see today who may be downcast, even though they appear to be cheerful and strong.

But God, who comforts the downcast, comforted us.
— 2 Corinthians 7:6 (NIV)

Seek God on behalf of **Europe and Central Asia**
Italy, Kazakhstan, Kosovo, Kyrgyzstan, Latvia, Liechtenstein, Lithuania, Luxembourg

SEEK GOD
...for freedom from terror

Day 30
THURSDAY
MARCH 10

*In righteousness you will be established.
You will be far from oppression,
for you will not fear;
and from terror,
for it will not come near you.*
— Isaiah 54:14

Come Prince of Peace! Reports of random violence in faraway lands have now become threats of impending terror close to home. In this darkened day, we see no right way to respond to the looming threat of evil. We stand with You in the singular goodness of Your righteousness. Your righteousness has already triumphed over hell itself. Give Your people a bold hope that under the influence of Your Lordship, there can once again be civil city life. Only such hope can withstand the fearsome force of terror itself. Established on the rock of Your righteousness, may our friendship overcome fear. As we obey You by loving neighbors as well as enemies, cause our kindness to become contagious.

*To grant us that we, being rescued
from the hand of our enemies,
might serve Him without fear,
in holiness and righteousness
before Him all our days.* — Luke 1:74-75

Give Your people a way to live uprightly for Your glory in wide-open, public ways. We have presumed that persecution is something long ago or far away. But now we face hostility. We cannot rescue ourselves. It is Yours to save. It is ours to serve. Establish Your people in the safety of following Christ in the virtue of His righteousness. Do not give us the beauty of His holiness apart from the vulnerability of His suffering. Grant Your people a way to worship and serve You fearlessly in the midst of reprisals so that Christ will be glorified.
Pray:

- For believers to live free from fear and to become peace-bearers in your city.
- That churches and believers worldwide would be delivered from persecution.

Seek God on behalf of **Fathers**

That fathers will look to God as the ultimate spiritual head of their household, serving and caring for their families; that God will instill a vision for wholesome, supportive fatherhood among the fathers of the city; that absentee fathers would change their lifestyles to nurture their wives and children; that children will see the character of the heavenly Father in the lives of their dads.

PRAYERWALK: Pray for the fathers in your workplace or near your home.

Fathers, do not exasperate your children; instead, bring them up in the training and instruction of the Lord.
— Ephesians 6:4 (NIV)

Seek God on behalf of **Europe and Central Asia**
Macedonia, Malta, Moldova, Monaco, Montenegro,
Netherlands, Norway, Poland, Portugal

SEEK GOD
...to establish righteous leaders

Day 31
FRIDAY
MARCH 11

*Then I will restore your judges
 as at the first,
and your counselors
 as at the beginning.
After that you will be called
 the city of righteousness, a faithful city.*
— Isaiah 1:26

You know the hearts of our leaders. They have hoped that right and wise governance would be a reality in our communities. You recognize their motives to desire the greatest good. But You also know how they may have been tempted or compromised. Grant them the humility of sober hope, a hope that guards against the worst of wickedness, but stubbornly aspires to the heights of Your righteousness. Restore their courage to do what may be unpopular. Purify their motives and give them strength to do the right things for all the right reasons. May our community become notorious for righteous and wise leaders. May it be acclaimed as a place of faithfulness.

Do not judge according to appearance, but judge with righteous judgment.
— John 7:24

Lord Jesus, our leaders are constantly pressured to please different groups and agendas. To prolong their power, they are tempted to tell white lies that are not clearly false, but are not really true. Lord of truth, fill them with the fear of God. Give them confidence in Your ways, so that they will act according to Your righteousness. *Pray:*

- For judges, court officials and lawmakers to fear God.
- For corruption to be purged from our justice system.
- For business leaders to pursue more than profits, but community-wide righteousness.

Seek God on behalf of **Agricultural Workers**

That God will abundantly bless families who farm, ranch or support agricultural industries; that they would follow Christ and find ways to be part of life-giving churches. Pray especially for migrant workers who sometimes face injustice and great difficulties.

PRAYERWALK: Pray in a rural area for God's blessing on the land and the families that He has placed there.

For the LORD your God will bless you in all your harvest and in all the work of your hands, and your joy will be complete.
— Deuteronomy 16:15 (NIV)

Seek God on behalf of **Europe and Central Asia**
Romania, Russia, San Marino, Serbia, Slovakia, Slovenia, Spain, Sweden

SEEK GOD
...for city-wide righteousness

Day 32
SATURDAY
MARCH 12

Sow with a view to righteousness,
reap in accordance with kindness.
Break up your fallow ground,
   for it is time to seek the LORD
   until He comes
   to rain righteousness on you.
— Hosea 10:12

For years fellow Christians have served our city in many ways. We envisioned tremendous moves of God following after our labors and prayers. But having done what we can, our city seems only slightly improved. How long until we see the harvest of transformation? We seek You, life-giving God. Visit our city with power and life from heaven, like a slow, steady rainfall. Cause our caring deeds to be as seeds that sprout to life and bear lasting fruit. Manifest Your vast presence, even in our small acts of kindness, so that many more come to seek You and the righteous life You give. Bring forth long-awaited seasons of city-wide righteousness.

But seek first His kingdom
   and His righteousness,
and all these things
will be added to you. — Matthew 6:33

As individual believers, we stand before You in the marvelous righteousness of Christ. But we want more than being right with You in a personal way. We desire Your kingdom and Your character throughout our community. This is not too much to hope for. Your jurisdiction already extends to all the streets, homes and businesses of our city. Cause many more to serve You as Lord and King. By their eager obedience cause Your kingdom to come so that Your will is actually done in the affairs of business, education and governance.
Pray:

- For believers to seek God's kingdom above all other things.
- For Christ's Lordship to change people in their personal life as well as in their public affairs.

Seek God on behalf of Arts and Entertainment

That God will inspire artists and entertainers with creativity and wisdom that reflect God's beauty; that they will seek God and come to follow Christ with courage; that their work will bring strength, goodness and hope to our communities.

PRAYERWALK: Visit an art museum, a theater, or a place of entertainment for the purpose of praying for the artists or those working in support capacities.

He has filled him with the Spirit of God, with skill, ability and knowledge in all kinds of crafts... to engage in all kinds of artistic craftsmanship.
— Exodus 35:31, 33 (NIV)

Seek God on behalf of Europe and Central Asia
Switzerland, Tajikistan, Turkmenistan, Ukraine, United Kingdom, Uzbekistan, Vatican City

Seeking His **Peace** Among **All Peoples**

MARCH 13-19 WEEK 5

Jesus did not promise that peace would prevail in this age. He actually assured us that there would be great conflicts until the end. Nevertheless, it is always right to pray for God to bring peace.

The peace of God is not the absence of war, it is the infusion of heaven's life on earth. Christ's peace is what love looks like, as people learn to walk in God's ways and live in His power. Although peace will not prevail in this age, we can be sure that the risen Lord is creating outbreaks of heaven's peace in every community as a sign that His kingdom is on the way.

The Middle East

During this fifth week, our prayers will be focused on the peoples, churches and countries of the Middle East.

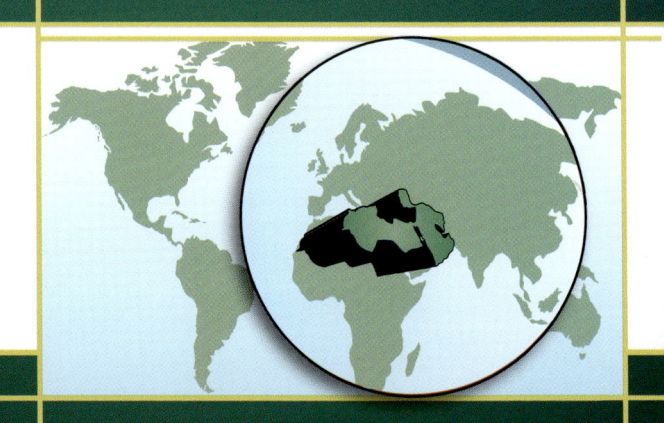

SEEK GOD
...for Christ to bless the nations with peace

Day 33
SUNDAY
MARCH 13

*In your seed
all the nations of the earth
shall be blessed,
because you have obeyed My voice.*
— Genesis 22:18

You disclosed Your purpose to Abraham, assuring him that You would bring about a marvelous destiny amidst every people. When this ancient purpose comes to be fulfilled, tangible blessing will abound in every language and lineage of humankind. The promise of Your blessing means that the story of every people will somehow culminate with exhibitions of the righteousness, peace and joy of Your kingdom. We ask You to bring forth the most basic blessing: Your peace, well-being and hope amidst every segment of our city. Increase this peace so that respect, honor and goodwill flows between the diverse peoples of our community.

*Your father Abraham rejoiced
to see My day, and he saw it
and was glad.* — John 8:56

Abraham saw You coming. He envisioned Your day, Lord Jesus. He rejoiced to see Your coming glory throughout all peoples, cultures and nations. Open the eyes of our hearts so that we, like Abraham so long ago, will envision the peace of Your kingdom in our midst. Give us faith to labor and pray, so that we become Your blessing in our city. Cause Your people to rejoice in glad confidence that Your peace will ultimately prevail. *Pray:*

- For respect, honor and goodwill to be formed between diverse peoples and races that live in your community.
- For culturally relevant churches to be planted among every ethnicity of your city.
- For Christ to bring reconciliation in the midst of racial tension.

Seek God on behalf of **the Military**

For the gospel to spread through the special relationships of military life; for courage and protection in the danger of battle; for wisdom and the fear of the Lord when military personnel are called upon to do the work of governing and enforcing law; for grace upon chaplains and other spiritual leaders; that God will fortify families stretched by numerous moves and separations.

PRAYERWALK: Pray near a military base or establishment.

A centurion came to Him, asking for help... When Jesus heard this, He was astonished and said..."I tell you the truth, I have not found anyone in Israel with such great faith."
— Matthew 8:5, 10 (NIV)

Seek God on behalf of **the Middle East**
Algeria, Bahrain, Cyprus

SEEK GOD
...for Christ to restore relationships

Day **34**
MONDAY
MARCH 14

I have hidden My face from this city because of all their wickedness: Behold, I will bring to it health and healing, and I will heal them; and I will reveal to them an abundance of peace...
  It will be to Me a name of joy, praise and glory before all the nations of the earth which will hear of all the good that I do for them.
– Jeremiah 33:5-6, 9

Many of our city have surmised that there will always be conflict between races, religions, genders and generations. Our family ties and our friendship bonds have weakened, blighted by the wickedness of selfish ambition and jealousy. We will never again turn toward each other if Your face remains turned away from us. Turn toward us, Lord God! Forgive our wickedness. Heal our broken souls. Persuade our cynical hearts that You can bring abundant peace. Do it for Your glory, Lord God. Become famous for bringing peace to our city.

If you had known in this day, even you, the things which make for peace!
  But now they have been hidden from your eyes. – Luke 19:42

In the hostilities of our city we can do little more than merely negotiate temporary truces. We have proven ourselves powerless to heal broken relationships. Only You, Lord Jesus, can change the hearts of people to bring forth heaven's peace. We are blind to what You bring, a grace that truly renews relationships of every kind. Lift the blinders from our eyes. Reveal Your ways and help us to walk in them. *Pray:*

- For hostile relationships to be reconciled in Christ.
- For believers to recognize God-given opportunities to make peace in their neighborhoods and networks.

Seek God on behalf of **Broken Families**

Pray for healing of broken or embittered relationships; for comfort when a family member has passed away. Pray that the Father heart of God will overshadow children, that they would know the joy of being part of God's family; that God will meet financial needs, bring supportive friends and grant hope to many who come to follow Christ.

PRAYERWALK: Apartment buildings often house fragmented families. Pray around an apartment complex, focusing prayers on those who have been bereaved or divorced.

The LORD...sustains the fatherless and the widow.
– Psalm 146:9 (NIV)

Seek God on behalf of **the Middle East**
Egypt, Iran, Iraq

SEEK GOD
...for God to restore children to their parents

Day 35
TUESDAY
MARCH 15

All your sons will be taught by the LORD, and great will be your children's peace.
– Isaiah 54:13 (NIV)

You have given parents the great responsibility to become the pattern that their children will follow. Even the best of parents in stable homes can fail to guide their children well. Children sometimes rebel with no apparent cause. So we approach You, our marvelous Father in heaven. Make Your presence known in our homes. Reconcile wayward parents to their children. Restore prodigal sons and daughters to their parents. Open our minds and lives to receive You as our teacher. And may Your peace be great in homes throughout our city.

And they were bringing children to Him so that He might touch them… And He took them in His arms and began blessing them, laying His hands on them.
– Mark 10:13, 16

When parents brought their kids to You, Lord Jesus, what kind of blessing did You pray? What did You bestow upon the little ones? What kind of hope for them was in Your heart? As we pray today, we bring the children of our city to You. Young or old, we still present them to You. We imagine You taking them in Your arms, healing their hearts and touching their inmost brokenness. Give us ways to speak Your words of blessing so that our children will fulfill Your highest desires. *Pray:*

- For parents to bless their children, speaking openly about God's plans for good in their lives.
- For daughters to live with single-minded zeal to love and serve Jesus.
- For sons to focus the passions of their hearts on Christ and His kingdom.

Seek God on behalf of **Laborers**

Pray that God will reveal the dignity and honor of doing work as unto Christ; that workplaces would be a setting of safety, joy and friendship; for workers to be treated with justice and dignity; for continued employment in the changing global economy; for many to follow Christ and serve Him openly in the workplace with co-laborers.

PRAYERWALK: Almost every community has factories, construction sites or other places of industry. Pray for the laborers in these places.

Blessed are all who fear the LORD, who walk in His ways. You will eat the fruit of your labor; blessings and prosperity will be yours.
– Psalm 128:1-2 (NIV)

Seek God on behalf of **the Middle East**
Israel, Jordan, Kuwait

SEEK GOD
...for enemies to be blessed

Day 36
WEDNESDAY
MARCH 16

When a man's ways are pleasing to the LORD, he makes even his enemies to be at peace with him.
– Proverbs 16:7

We like to think that we have no personal enemies. But in fact we avoid the ones we fear and ignore the ones we have wronged. We have often failed at making peace. Left on our own, we will only succeed in defending ourselves. We want to please You in all of our relationships. Do more than just forgive us; empower us to forgive. Train us in Your ways. Reform our attitudes. Give us hearts to bless the ones who may have harmed us. Grant us favor, even with those hostile to us, and cause us to live in peacemaking ways that please You.

But I say to you, love your enemies and pray for those who persecute you, so that you may be sons of your Father who is in heaven.
– Matthew 5:44-45

Even as Your enemies nailed You to a cross, You cried out for God to forgive them. In our day we see enemies of the cross rising up with alarming strength. Make us to be Your sons and daughters who prove Your love by enduring the hostility of those who hate You with prayers of blessing. Give these, Your enemies, what none of us deserve: the forgiveness and blessing of Your love. *Pray:*

- That believers would love and pray for their enemies.
- For those who oppose Christ to experience His mercy.
- For Christians suffering under oppressive governments to remain faithful, in all things following Christ's example.

Seek God on behalf of the Athletic Industry

Pray for those in support roles and those with higher profiles, that they will know Christ and fulfill God's calling in their lives. Pray that athletes would be good examples of dedication, commitment and courage; that they will live with integrity and carry out the responsibility of wealth and reputation; that God will reveal His calling and purpose for students and coaches in high school and university programs.

PRAYERWALK: Pray on-site at the scene of an upcoming sports event near you.

Yours, O LORD, is the greatness and the power and the glory... Wealth and honor come from You... In Your hands are strength and power to exalt and give strength to all.
–1 Chronicles 29:11-12 (NIV)

Seek God on behalf of the Middle East
Lebanon, Libya, Morocco

SEEK GOD
...to calm the storm of war

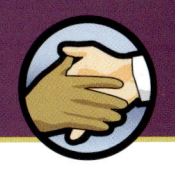

Day 37
THURSDAY
MARCH 17

He will judge between the nations, and
*　will render decisions for many peoples*
and they will hammer
*　　their swords into plowshares and*
*　　their spears into pruning hooks.*
Nation will not lift up sword
*　against nation,*
and never again will they learn war.
— Isaiah 2:4

Intervene by Your authority in the affairs of the nations. Calm the storm of war that rolls across the face of the earth. Accomplish what thousands of diplomats could never achieve. Isaiah's promise speaks of what You will do at the very end of the age. But we dare to ask that in our day You will move to bring an outbreak of peace that will signify, in a momentous way, the peace of the age to come. As You bring an end to relatively small conflicts in our city, reveal Yourself as the powerful peacemaking King that You are.

In His name the nations
will put their hope.
— Matthew 12:21 (NIV)

For many reasons, people from many nations have arrived in our city. Some have come with dreams of prosperity and peace. Others are exiles and refugees, with lingering anger and despair. Disappointment affects them all, despite the best intentions of nice neighbors and appointed leaders. May this be the time, Lord Jesus, that the nations look to You. And may this city be the place where You are seen to be the sole hope of the nations. Reveal Yourself now by Your Spirit so that families, clans and entire peoples are moved to hope in You. *Pray:*

- For God to resolve racial or ethnic conflicts that may persist in your city.
- That people from distant lands who reside in your community will come to encounter the hope that is in Jesus.

Seek God on behalf of **Ethnic Communities**

That God will bring racial harmony; that long-standing offenses may be healed by the forgiveness that begins in Jesus; that Christians show honor and act in Christ's reconciling power; that the beauty of distinctive languages and cultures would be on display in local churches.

PRAYERWALK: Pray blessings in a neighborhood with an ethnic identity different than your own, or pray blessings upon a business owned by people of another ethnicity than yours.

All the ends of the earth will remember and turn to the LORD, and all the families of the nations will bow down before Him.
— Psalm 22:27 (NIV)

Seek God on behalf of **the Middle East**
Oman, Qatar, Saudi Arabia

SEEK GOD
...to gather all peoples in worship

Day 38
FRIDAY
MARCH 18

This will be written
  for the generation to come,
  that a people yet to be created
  may praise the LORD...
when the peoples are gathered together,
and the kingdoms, to serve the LORD.
— Psalm 102:18, 22

What has been promised must be fulfilled: You will save and create a people from all peoples. Since the day Christ rose from the dead You have been forming this new body of worshipers. This global people will name You with praise that resonates throughout the earth. We long to hear that song. But at this hour we are not yet gathered as one people. We still find ourselves separated and segregated in our cities. Hear us as we unite our prayers. Look with favor upon us as we gather to serve You in worship. Assemble us before You as one family drawn together from many peoples.

He began to teach and say to them, "Is it not written: 'My house will be called a house of prayer for all nations.'"
— Mark 11:17

Lord Jesus, continue what You began to teach us. Correct our jaded and stale ideas about worship. Instruct our hearts so that we blaze with hope for the destiny of all peoples. The global people You are forming will become so diverse and numerous that we will never fit in any of our church buildings. Be pleased with our humble gatherings, but form us to be a global house, made without hands, coming together as summoned from every culture, language and race. Call diverse assemblies of the peoples to worship You together in the beauty of truth and in the fullness of Your Spirit. As we come to You, make Your home with us. *Pray:*

- For city-wide worship events that bring the community together in festivals of praise.
- For churches divided by different traditions to experience unity in worshiping Jesus.

Seek God on behalf of **the Unborn**

That these precious children will be acknowledged and honored by all; for each one to find sheltering homes; that the awful waste of their lives would cease; that they would come to Christ at an early age; for the parents of unborn babies, that God will turn their hearts toward their children.

PRAYERWALK: As you pray for your neighbors, pray that God will break the power of self-centered lifestyles that disregard children, and that He will forgive and heal those who have harmed their children in any way.

For He will deliver... the afflicted who have no one to help. He will...save the needy from death. He will rescue them from oppression and violence, for precious is their blood in His sight.
— Psalm 72:12-14 (NIV)

Seek God on behalf of **the Middle East**
Syria, Tunisia, Turkey

SEEK GOD
...for Christ's Lordship to be welcomed by the nations

Day 39
SATURDAY
MARCH 19

Rejoice greatly, O daughter of Zion!
Shout in triumph, O daughter of Jerusalem!
Behold, your king is coming to you.
   He is just and endowed with salvation,
   humble, and mounted on a donkey...
And the bow of war will be cut off.
And He will speak peace to the nations;
and His dominion will be from sea to sea.
— Zechariah 9:9-10

Before You come to bring an end to the age, You will come in triumphant humility, to bring a better salvation than anyone expected. Your voice will be lifted up, somehow speaking so that everyone will hear. What You say will be gentle, disarming evil powers without conventional weapons. Already many have heard Your voice. Already You have been speaking peace in the midst of war. We welcome You as You come to our community. Without waging a war of conquest, You have already conquered our hearts. You will soon be utterly victorious over evil. Come magnificent King! Our hope is fixed on You.

And as Jesus returned,
   the people welcomed Him,
   for they had all been waiting for Him.
— Luke 8:40

We cannot know when You will come again, but find us waiting expectantly when You do. We are not merely waiting for the end of all things. Instead, we are waiting for You to begin all things that last and matter. And that's why we do more than wait for You. We welcome You. As an act of love, we welcome You. May our expectancy incite others of our community to receive You. May there be many in our city who love Your kingdom and Your appearing. Even so, come, Lord Jesus. *Pray:*

- That Jesus will be expected and loved by many who wait eagerly for His return.
- For a visitation of Christ's peace-bringing presence to be welcomed by millions across the face of the earth.

Seek God on behalf of **Elderly People**

That God's strength and peace will be poured out on everyone who is advanced in years. Pray that they may be honored, that they may be cared for; that loneliness be banished through lasting friendships and family bonds; that sickness be lifted; that they may live to see their prayers answered; that their latter years will be significant, reflecting the glory of God.

PRAYERWALK: Pray for the oldest person you know in your neighborhood. Or pray at a retirement community or an extended care facility.

Now Abraham was old, advanced in age; and the LORD had blessed Abraham in every way.
— Genesis 24:1

Seek God on behalf of **the Middle East**
United Arab Emirates, Yemen

Seeking His **Visitation**
Welcoming Christ our King

MARCH 20 PALM SUNDAY

> The event we have come to call "Palm Sunday" shines as a prophetic portrait of the spiritual awakening Christ desires to bring.

The event we have come to call "Palm Sunday" shines as a prophetic portrait of the spiritual awakening Christ desires to bring. Jesus not only initiated the procession, but He refused to shut it down. He was doing more than merely fulfilling prophecy. He was prophesying, presenting a lasting vision of how He will be recognized in the midst of hostility at the end of the age. Christ will be followed by some in every people. He will be welcomed, at least by a few, in every place. Palm Sunday gives us a vision of the global spiritual awakening we are praying toward.

Preparing the way by prayer

Jesus prepared the way for Palm Sunday by sending His followers to pray on-site in many communities (Luke 10:1-2). The prayers of these ordinary followers were publicly prayed and then openly answered. God was being honored. Jesus was becoming famous in places where He had not yet personally visited. The expectancy of what God would do was great.

A crescendo of welcoming praise

The raising of Lazarus touched off an explosion of welcoming praise (John 12:18). The dramatic answer to Jesus' prayer for His friend Lazarus (John 11:41-43) got everyone talking about all they had seen God do in the lives of their friends and neighbors. Luke says the crowd was praising God "for all the miracles which they had seen" (Luke 19:37). Grateful praise for many answered prayers quickly became a crescendo of welcoming worship.

Palm Sunday: The hope of Christ's visitation

A lasting movement

Thousands of people gathered at the temple with Jesus early every morning, hanging on His every word (Luke 21:38). The Palm Sunday worshipers should not be confused with the much smaller mob which shouted for Jesus' execution later in the week. That crowd was incited by Christ's enemies, who were forced to arrest Jesus by night "because they were afraid of the people" —the very throng that had welcomed and honored Him daily with increasing devotion (Luke 22:2, Mark 14:1-2).

A prophetic portrait

Palm Sunday is sometimes dismissed as if it were a political rally gone wrong. But Jesus was all for it. He planned whatever could have been planned. And He refused to silence the celebration. He said that rocks would have cried out if the people had been restrained (Luke 19:40). The intensity mounted. The crowds increased. Eventually "all the city was stirred, saying, 'Who is this?'" (Matthew 21:10). Those who hadn't yet personally encountered Jesus were eager to know more. If Jesus was giving us any indication of how God desires to visit communities with transforming power, we are right in praying for such receptive glory to sweep throughout whole cities.

The hope of visitation: His arrival more than our revival

Hated or praised, Christ was then what He will be again: the sole focus of attention of whole cities in days of great spiritual awakening. Our best prayers are prayers of welcome—that the risen Jesus Himself will be recognized and received throughout entire communities. Whenever there has been revival, it has been a partial fulfillment of the promise of Palm Sunday. Now, more than ever, it's time to invite Christ the Lord to bring His life-giving presence upon our cities.

> **Whenever there has been revival, it has been a partial fulfillment of the promise of Palm Sunday.**

Day 40

PALM SUNDAY
MARCH 20

SEEK GOD
...for Christ to visit our communities

On the first Palm Sunday, the crowds shouted phrases from Psalm 118, which was one of the songs traditionally sung at the Passover holiday. Jesus had been rejected as the Messiah before then, but on that day He was put on display. Many honored and received Him, while others confirmed their rejection. But no one ignored Him. Suddenly, it became clear that the Almighty God was visiting with transforming power.

> The stone the builders rejected
>   has become the capstone.
> The LORD has done this,
>   and it is marvelous in our eyes.
> This is the day the LORD has made.
> Let us rejoice and be glad in it. — Psalm 118:22-24

Many have repudiated Your Son, but bring a day in our community when Jesus will be honored and received by many, even if others still reject Him. Open our eyes to recognize what You have done to exalt Your Son as Lord of all the earth. May the Lordship of Christ become such an abounding reality that we find ourselves rejoicing in Your day of finishing fullness.

Many suddenly saw that they could be saved in ways they never thought possible before. They could see You accelerating Your purpose toward Your intended goal. The cry, "Hosanna!" was a way of saying, "We're saved!" and at the same time, a way of asking for the fullest purpose of His salvation to be fulfilled.

> O LORD, save us! [literally: hosanna]
> O LORD, push things forward to finish.
>   Blessed is He who comes
>   in the name of the LORD. — Psalm 118:25-26 (Translation by author)

Open our eyes to see Jesus coming to our city. Awaken hope that He will save us more than we've ever been saved. We say, "Yes!" to Him. We welcome Him now with joy. He has come, but He will yet come, to reveal the name and glory of God.

More than anything else, Palm Sunday was a day in which God revealed His Son. It stands as a fact behind us, but it also looms large and beautiful before us, as a promise of Christ's visitation.

> The LORD is God, and He has given us light. — Psalm 118:27

Lord God, give us light so that Jesus becomes utterly marvelous in our eyes. Make us strong in hope and eager in expectancy. Give light to many throughout our city, so that Jesus will be welcomed, followed and loved.

...with His presence and transforming power

*When He came near...the whole crowd of disciples
began joyfully to praise God in loud voices
for all the miracles they had seen:
"Blessed is the king who comes
in the name of the Lord!
Peace in heaven and glory in the highest!"*
— Luke 19:37-40 (NIV)

On Palm Sunday, many people had not only heard, but had also seen with their eyes, miraculous answers to prayer that were done in Your name. There was joy because You were recognized as more than a miracle-worker. Somehow it became clear that God was exalting You to lead the entire human race as King. You have come, not by campaign or by conquest. You come in the name of the everlasting God, to be our King. You are the Lord.

Be welcomed in our city in the same way You were received on Palm Sunday. Many people had tasted the sweet freedom of the gospel of Your kingdom. They had seen Your humble might in overcoming evil powers. They raised their voices exclaiming You as altogether unique. They loved the idea of You as their Lord.

Do such great things, wondrous things, in our city. Act in answer to prayers in Your name. Heal, restore and reconcile. Make people different in ways that defy simple explanations. Move in ways that are open and public, that cannot be dismissed. Bring about a groundswell of open praise. And may the peace of Your kingdom in our city be as great as Your glory in heaven.

Even so, come, Lord Jesus.

Seek God on behalf of
The Coming Generation

When the chief priests and the scribes saw ... the children who were shouting in the temple, "Hosanna to the Son of David," they became indignant and said to Him, "Do You hear what these children are saying?" And Jesus said to them, "Yes; have you never read, 'Out of the mouth of infants...You have prepared praise for Yourself'?"
— Matthew 21:15-16

That many who are now small children would soon become passionate followers of Christ; that during their lifetimes they will finish evangelizing the world; that they will endure suffering to overcome evil and bring forth the promised blessing of God upon all peoples; that they will give Christ the finest whole-life worship of all history.

PRAYERWALK: **Walk your city thinking of the people who will live there in years to come, should the Lord delay His second coming. Pray for the generation that will be dwelling in your city when Christ returns.**

---

*Seek God
on behalf of*
Jerusalem

Pray for God's peace and glory to be upon Jerusalem.

Co-working with God in the story of His love

God's persistent kindness
by Steve Sjogren with Steve Hawthorne

When did God begin to do good things in your life? Was it only after you became a Christian?

Actually, the Bible is very clear about God doing good things in people's lives long before they even know about Him. There's a story of kindness in every person's life. God delights in showing His premeditated, forever love with tangible acts of kindness. Here's why: The Bible says that "the kindness of God leads you to repentance" (Romans 2:4).

God's kindness never coerces us. Instead, His goodness "leads" us through the events of our lives to the point where we can turn, or repent. God will never force people to turn around. We have to do our own turning.

Follow God's great desire. God is motivated with unstoppable passion to regain relationship with people. He deeply "desires" that "all people" would "come to the knowledge of the truth" about Him (1 Timothy 2:4). Knowing the truth about God can open a relationship with Him. That's what being "saved" is all about.

Co-work with God. Because of His constant desire for every single person to know Him, God gives us two simple but powerful ways to work with Him:

   1. Pray for every person. God wants us to pray for every person. "First of all, I urge that...prayers, petitions and thanksgiving be made on behalf of all people" (1 Timothy 2:1).

   2. Convey and display the message with perfect timing. God gives us opportunity to make clear the message about Jesus with divine timing, "the testimony [to be] given in its proper time" (1 Timothy 2:6).

Our part isn't hard.
Caring prayers, tangible kindness and well-timed words

Why pray at all? There's joy in it. God doesn't need our prayers to act. He doesn't really need our efforts to serve people. But He does want us to experience the joy of co-working with Him (and with others who are praying with us!) in bringing new life to others. As you keep attentive to what God may be doing, don't be surprised if God opens opportunities for you to express His love in tangible ways.

Pray along with what God is already doing. Since God's work is always a story, your best praying will be part of an ongoing story. Instead of using prayer as a quick-fix procedure that supposedly gets results if performed correctly, your prayer is a way of collaborating with God.

God is already on the move. Prayer does not push God to get started. He's already doing good things in everyone's life. And He desires to do even better things. Instead of holding off the worst, think of your prayers as asking God to bring on the best.

Persistent, life-giving **prayer** for others leads to opportunities to **care,** displaying God's love, which opens the way to **share** the gospel, declaring God's love.

A simple sequence: Prayer-Care-Share.
On the following pages, we (Steve Sjogren and Steve Hawthorne) offer some proven ideas for how you can pray for others. As you pay attention and take notice of what God may be doing in their lives, you'll often find that there are simple ways for you to do small acts of kindness that can reveal God's great love. Putting God's love on display often opens ways to present the gospel with sensitivity and clarity.

Life-giving prayer

Pray your way into their story

There's a story rolling in everyone's life. God has done and will do good things in people's lives. He does good things long before anyone opens their life to Christ.

It's the kindness of God that leads anyone to repentance (Romans 2:4). Meeting, following and serving Christ is always a lifelong story. The typical stories have multiple encounters and experiences that turn people closer to or further from Christ. Someone researching effective ways to lead people to Christ found that most people have no less than five significant encounters in which the message of the gospel registers at the heart level.

As we connect with people in practical ways, those deep heart connections increase rapidly. I love to assume that God is on the verge of doing something good in the lives of everyone I see in order to bring about yet one more significant encounter with His love. I enjoy getting in on the story by praying my way, or "noticing" my way into what God may be up to next.

Praying for people is the simplest way I know to start seeing them from God's point of view—to notice what they're facing or to get a hunch about what God may have underway.

Prayer *leads to* **care**

Prayerwalk
to get in step with what God is doing

When we live at too fast a pace, we can miss God's invitations to become part of the story He's unfolding in people's lives. Prayerwalking is a way to slow down and begin to naturally pick up on the concerns of God. His heart begins to merge with ours. We allow what causes Him excitement or anguish to affect us in the same way.

Prayerwalking is praying near the people you are praying for, in the places where they live or work. Prayerwalking isn't really about walking around. It's praying with your eyes and heart wide open so you can take notice of what God may be wanting to do in their lives. You can pray quietly with your eyes open without people necessarily knowing that you are praying for them. Be on the scene without making one.

What to pray
You don't have to have an official "prayer request" to start praying creatively. Try praying in these three ways:

1. **Thank your way into God's story.** How has God provided, protected or guided them? We're told to offer "thanksgiving on behalf of all people" (1 Timothy 2:1). When you think about it, it's not hard to do. What you're doing is "noticing" what God may be doing. Such "noticing" makes it easier to pray and easier to see what part God may give you in what's coming next.

2. **Notice what they may be facing.** What fears, pain or ambitions are driving them? What relationships or disappointments have paralyzed them? What turmoil or crisis may be overwhelming them? Pray accordingly.

3. **Pray with scripture.** Check out the passages of scripture in the side margins of the pages throughout this booklet. Many of them can give you ideas about what you can pray.

opening ways to **share** the gospel.

Practical ways to care.

From noticing to nudging

A small kindness can show great love

As you pray for others, "noticing" what God is doing in their lives, you allow God to point out needs as well as opportunities. It's as if He is "noticing" through you.

Often, those needs work as your cue that it's your time to play a bit part in the story. In the flow of what is unfolding in people's lives, God uses small acts of kindness to reveal the great love of Christ.

Kindness is never accidental. It's always intentional. Get creative. Team up with others. Dream up ways to serve people in small, tangible ways. You might call it committing acts of non-random kindness.

Many fear sharing the gospel because they think that they'll have to be pushy. No one likes pushy people. So don't be pushy. Instead of pushing, your act of kindness may "nudge" them closer to the time when they will open their life to Christ. Those around me are gaining courage as they see how uncomplicated it all is. Just show God's love in small ways and see where it goes.

Great resources for many more good ideas
Steve Sjogren has developed some good resources designed to help ordinary people show God's love in practical ways. He has hundreds of tested ideas. Go to **www.KindnessResources.com**.

"I highly recommend Steve's resources. He makes it fun." —Steve Hawthorne

Prayer *leads to* care

Demonstrate
God's love in a practical way

Nudging people with God's love can be done thousands of ways. It's God's love. You don't have to feel it. Just find some simple way to display the smallest kindness. I define it this way: Demonstrate the kindness of God by offering to do some act of humble service with no strings attached.

For people near you who know you
Show your concern naturally by doing "golden rule" kindness: Do something for others that you are already going to do for yourself. Almost any simple errand you can do at work or household chore can be extended to those you know. Some ideas:

- **Watch the kids.** Offer to watch your neighbor's kids so they can do some errands or just take a break.
- **Write a note.** Birthday, holiday, or figure out something to thank them for.
- **Move the cans.** Drag their garbage cans back off the street on trash day.
- **Buy extra flowers.** "Accidentally" on purpose buy too many flowers for your home and bring some to a neighbor.
- **Shovel the driveway.** Clear the snow for someone else before you do yours.
- **Bake too many.** Bake cookies. Make enough to share.
- **Go for coffee.** If you're going for coffee, ask if you can get some for a co-worker. Or just surprise them. A week later they may want to go along with you to talk.

For people you don't know — yet
Team up with others to display some kindness in a public setting to people you've never met. Do it with no strings attached and without any sermons. Just do helpful things. Always explain what you are doing by saying something like: "We're doing a free community service project to show God's love in a practical way." Conversations will get going easily. You'll have fun and be able to notice what God may be doing in their lives.

Distribute inexpensive but helpful stuff like cool drinks or popsicles when it's hot. Or provide a simple service that can be done quickly such as washing windows, raking leaves, cleaning toilets, clearing gutters, washing cars and hundreds more.

opening ways to **share** the gospel.

Engaging ways to share
Connecting the stories

Listening in order to tell

As you "notice" your way into the story of people's lives by sincerely serving them or praying for them, you'll become convinced that there are new chapters and better endings in their story than they may have ever dreamed.

How do you tell them about it? It's tempting to think that you have to tell or sell the gospel as a powerful, sermon-like speech. Instead of blasting away, do some "story-listening." That can turn into "story-exchanging," which leads to the best gospel story-telling.

I've been watching for the moments that God makes to convey even a little bit of the gospel. It takes the pressure off and puts it on God. Even small bits of banter with people can unfold into some amazing conversations. He really is present in their life story, even as we talk.

It's fun to point out what God may have already been doing in their lives, to explain how they can know Him better. And nudge them on their way.

Many avoid evangelism because it usually puts pressure on those who speak and those who listen. It gets clouded with fear and guilt on both sides.

Prayer *leads to* **care,**

Relate
the gospel story with their story

Connecting may be easier than you think

I find that many hesitate to do what I call "crossing over" into other people's lives. It's really a matter of engaging in conversations. Usually the "crossing over" never happens because we are waiting for some kind of open door to spontaneously happen. That's just too much waiting. While we wait for God to open doors, we will often find that He's already unlocked them.

Try doing this: Make up an excuse to connect with people. Sometimes I borrow things from people even when I don't really need anything. At work I have borrowed paper or a pen or a stapler for an hour. Upon returning the item, it is natural to engage in a few minutes of conversation. With neighbors I've borrowed ingredients (for the cookies I bring over later), or tools that I may not urgently need. The key is to find a reason to "stop on by." It may be to borrow something, or it may be to give them something. You might never know your neighbors if you don't "stop on by."

Watch for three stories

God is bringing together His story with their story. Watch how three stories intersect and overlap:

- **Their story.** How do they tell their own story? Keep listening to what's important to them.
- **Your own "Jesus story."** By your own "Jesus story" I mean the saga of how God has been doing things in your life that brought you into relationship with Jesus. As you know, that story is still unfolding. You are still being changed by Christ.
- **The gospel story.** By the gospel story I mean what God has been doing in lives, cities and nations through the ages. It's a story, of course, that centers on what Christ has done, is doing and will do. There are hundreds of ways to tell God's story.

Find ways to get into conversations with others about their life and their story. Listen well and you'll find ways that your story corresponds to something of theirs. You'll find it natural to exchange parts of your story with theirs. You can explain how Jesus has come to play a major role in your life. From there it's not hard to tell the greater gospel story as you have come to know Christ and walk with Him.

opening ways to **share** the gospel.

PRAYERCONNECT

Connecting to the heart of Christ through prayer

A 32-page magazine designed to:

Equip prayer leaders and pastors
with tools to disciple their congregations.

Connect intercessors
with the growing worldwide prayer movement.

Mobilize believers to pray God's purposes
for their church, city and the nations.

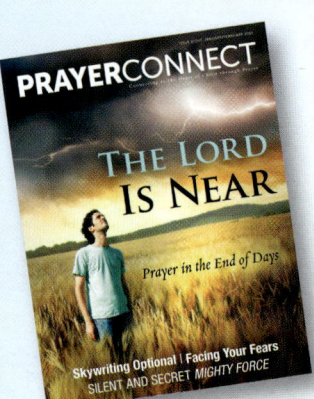

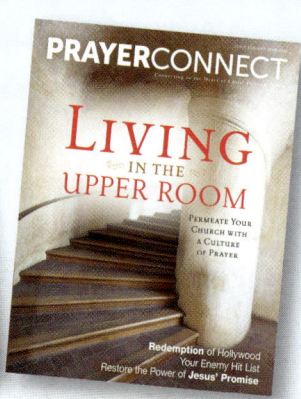

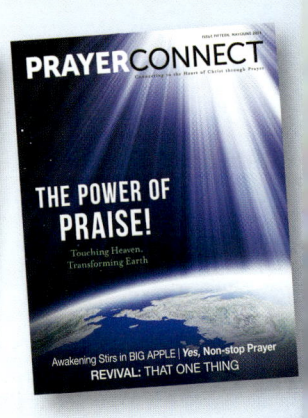

Each issue of **PRAYER**CONNECT includes:

- Practical articles to equip and inspire your prayer life.
- Helpful prayer tips and proven ideas.
- News of prayer movements around the world.
- Theme articles exploring important prayer topics.
- Connections to prayer resources available online.

Three different ways to subscribe *(five issues a year)*:

$24.99 - **Print** *(includes digital version)*
$19.99 - **Digital**
$30.00 - **Membership** in Church Prayer Leaders Network
(includes print, digital and CPLN benefits)

Subscribe now.
Order at www.prayerconnect.net or call 800-217-5200.

PRAYERCONNECT is sponsored by: America's National Prayer Committee, Denominational Prayer Leaders Network and The International Prayer Council.

Praying with faith, hope and love for our Muslim neighbors

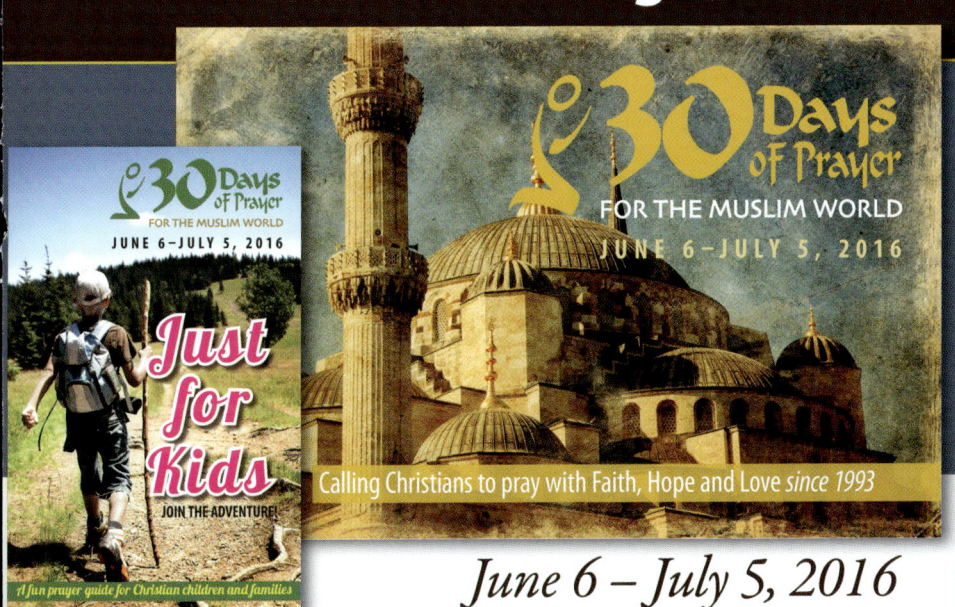

30 Days of Prayer
FOR THE MUSLIM WORLD
JUNE 6 – JULY 5, 2016

Just for Kids
JOIN THE ADVENTURE!
A fun prayer guide for Christian children and families

30 Days of Prayer
FOR THE MUSLIM WORLD
JUNE 6 – JULY 5, 2016

Calling Christians to pray with Faith, Hope and Love *since 1993*

June 6 – July 5, 2016

The 25th Edition

30 Days of Prayer *for the* Muslim World

Join millions of Christians around the world who participate each year in this largest ongoing international prayer focus on the Muslim world.

Coinciding with Ramadan, Christians worldwide are called to make an intentional effort to learn about, pray for and reach out to Muslim neighbors —across the street and around the world.

Media sound bites about Islamic extremism can too easily incite anger, fear and even hatred toward Muslims. Instead, pray with the mind and heart of Christ. This full-color prayer guide —available in both adult and kids versions—is a proven tool helping Christians to understand and to persistently pray for Muslim neighbors and nations.

To order, or to learn more, go to:
www.30DaysPrayer.com
Or email:
paulf@30DaysPrayer.com
Or write:
**WorldChristian.com "30 Days"
PO Box 9208
Colorado Springs, CO 80932**

WORLDCHRISTIAN.COM
Resources and Ministry that Impact Our World

30 Days of Prayer
PRAYING FOR OUR WORLD